It Is Hard to be Humble!
When You Own a Borzoi

Gabrielle Slater

It Is Hard to be Humble!

Chapter 1

How did all this start?

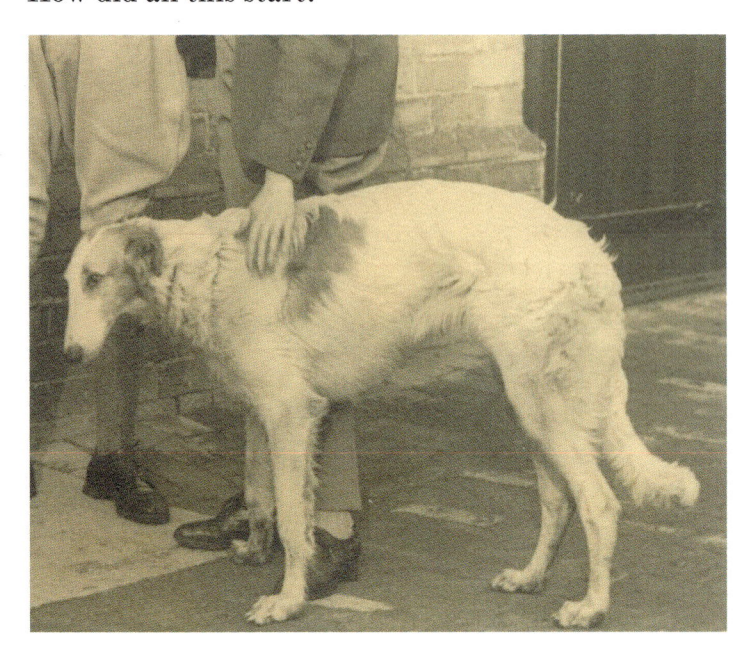

I wish I knew. Possibly, I can blame my mother, she had had Ivan, in the 1930's, who died, she told me, from jaundice. I just thought he sounded wonderful and from a small child, I wanted a Borzoi. Mother said NO.
She was given a whippet, by the local farmer, who I fell in love with and, Martha became my first dog. I became infatuated by whippets, but in my heart of hearts, the illusive Borzoi was what I craved for.
Many years later, when I married, I tested this out on my new husband, the answer was still no!
Early in my married life, he took me to the New Forest for a few days. Walking the whippets one afternoon, I met this magical creature, this wonderful breed of dog I had longed for, for so long, but never met.
I was completely captivated, my instinct had been right … … I had to own a Borzoi … … but how?
My chance came unexpectedly, so often it does! All my life, I had lived a few miles from where I had been born. My husband saw the chance to move away, all be it only 20 miles, but … … it was out of my sheltered little area. It was a beautiful house, with 200 acres of farm land, which is what he wanted, ideal for the whippets, but I could see the deal!!!!!!!!
I don't want to move, I said, can't bare to go outside my little area … Well, OK, I will go, on one condition, I want a Borzoi. To my utter amazement, he agreed, on condition we moved and settled in first. How could I argue?
Having more or less settled, with my two whippets, I bought a dog paper and from that, found my first Borzoi advertised. I bought her, a pretty red bitch, who was already named Bubbly. How I loved her. My life with Borzoi had begun.

Chapter 2, Bubbly's Story

What a sweet bitch, I adored her and after all these years, I still find it very hard to write about her.

She was wonderful, perfect, just my dream come true, my first Borzoi. Mother used to get upset by her name. "How can you call a Russian dog Bubbly, she should be called Vodka"! But Bubbly she was, in more ways than one … It suited her.

I used to let her, with the whippets, run free and chase hares, I became friendly with the neighbouring farmer to our 200 acres and he was more than happy to let me do this with my dogs and let them run free on his land as well. So for a short time, she had an idyllic life.

Then came the day that my husband wanted a holiday, so we booked to go to Jersey for a week. We employed what I really believed, was a trustworthy person, to come into the house to look after our dogs. Knowing that Bubbly was a bit wild, I decided, that for one week, she could remain on a lead, so much so, that incase she lost the lead, I made several more, out of binder twine, as a backup.

On our second night in Jersey, we were called to the telephone. Our local police had rung, to tell us that Bubbly had been run over and killed. My husband would not let me return home, I was distraught and for the rest of our holiday, I wept. The one good thing he did for me, was to make sure, the lady concerned was out of the house before I got home. I learnt from our police, she never once put her on a lead. At night, she and my whippets, were put out the door and just left to roam. The lady concerned, is dead now, but from that day to the day she died, I never spoke to her again. A sweet bitch, cut down in her prime by one woman's laziness.

As time went by, I knew I had to have another Borzoi, so nervously, I contacted Bubbly's breeder. Quite rightly, he was pretty sharp with me. News travels fast in the Borzoi world and he thought I had been responsible for letting her roam.

He told me, he had no puppies but, he was prepared to let me have Bubbly's mum, Undomeil Blestka of Matalona, or Bessie.

Chapter 3, Bessie's Story

I was lucky, in the fact that this Borzoi kennel was not too far from where we were living. What had happened to Bubbly was making me nervous of having another, I wanted Bessie desperately, but could I trust myself enough to try again. Bubbly had been a puppy but, this was a five year old bitch, set in her ways and devoted to her breeder. Even taking her for a walk was a problem, she pulled so hard on her lead, I could hardly hang on to her. I just wasn't sure.

I would go and see her, several times a week, but just couldn't make my mind up to say yes. Eventually, after about a month of this, it was made up for me, I literally fell into the trap! One morning, when I had gone to see her, the breeder said he would be interested to see where we lived, fare enough, if I was going to have his dog, he should see where she would be going to live. He told me he would follow me in his car, so that I wouldn't have to drive him back, this sounded reasonable. He said he would like to bring a few of his dogs with him, so that they could have a walk on fresh ground, reasonable, I thought. He piled a load of dogs into his car and I took Bessie in mine, with my two whippets. The trap had been set!

We had a pleasant morning with all the dogs, walking and playing with them, then I asked him into the house. He put his dogs back into his car, and he and Bessie came inside. I was amazed how well Bessie settled, very quickly making herself at home, in an arm chair. About an hour or so later, he said he must be getting home. He got up and went to the door, Bessie didn't move, I called her, to come off the chair, Bessie became deaf! What about Bessie? I called after him, as he was getting into the car. Oh! I can't take her, there's no room in the car for another one. The trap was sprung! I had been caught, Bessie was mine! There was no question of whether she would settle in, she had!

A black cloud began to loom on the horizon. The breeder had failed to tell me, that she had recently been mated and that he wanted her back, to whelp, with him. I did not realise what agony this would cause.

With a heavy heart, I took her back to him, just a couple of days before she was due. When I left her that day, I could hear her howls as I drove away. At his suggestion, I stayed away, until after her litter of fourteen were born. I couldn't wait to go and see her again. It was agony, I thought she would be so happy with her new family, but no, when she saw me, she charged out of her whelping box, scattering her enormous litter everywhere, she jumped up, she cried, she screamed and covered my face with licks, she was demented. Leaving her was Hell, for her and for me, her cries were dreadful.

I did this trip daily, except weekends, when my husband was home, as he liked me there and, I didn't want to upset the apple cart for the future. Yes, I was beginning to think ahead!

Then, one terrible morning, when I got there, things were not as they should be. Bessie was cowering and there was a definite bad atmosphere. It was my fault, my visits had upset her, in the night, she had laid on and squashed one of the pups. She was to be punished, never to see her litter again; I was to take her home.

I cannot now remember how old they were but I do know, far too young to leave their mum. I felt dreadful, all my fault. I was ignorant in those days, but now I know, to raise a litter of fourteen, in the tiny whelping box she was in, without lying on one, was virtually impossible, now I am amazed that she didn't lie on more.

I was mortified, all my fault, but the joy of taking her home, knew no bounds, but there was worse to come.

Bessie was so full of milk, it was agony for her. It took a long and expensive veterinary treatment, to make her comfortable again.

I never knew what became of that litter, at the time, I did not know any Borzoi people, and now that I do, prefer not to know.

There was one lighter moment during this time. I used to visit Edith, a wonderful old lady, in her late 80s/early 90/s, who had been crippled in a car crash – she was wheelchair bound, but very independent, living in a ground floor flat in my local town. She loved dogs; I took both Bubbly and later, Bessie to see her, when I went to visit her. She was distraught when Bubbly was killed and, a great comfort to me.

I told the breeder, at some point, about her and, one day, before the puppy squashing incident, he suggested to me, that we put Bessie and her litter in my car and take them to her. With experience, not a good idea, but it made one lovely, lonely little woman so happy.

One day, I took my then small daughter, my whippet and Bessie, to a local agricultural show. As we wandered round the various stands and stalls, I noticed a dog show was about to start, we decided to enter Bessie. In those days, I knew absolutely nothing about showing dogs; the age of innocence you could call it! I went to the table to collect an entry form, horror of horror's; you had to pick your class. Any variety sporting or, any variety nonsporting, what on earth was Bessie? In the end, I had to ask. A very superior lady looked down her nose at me. "Bred to hunt wolves wasn't she? So sporting of course". I remember wanting to retort, "Not her, no wolves around here!" I have never seen so many different shapes and sizes that were in that class. Gundogs, Terriers, Hounds, I lost my nerve and sent daughter in with Bessie! I sat by the ringside with the whippet and waited and waited, it seemed to go on forever. Eventually, the judge, standing in earshot of me, announced to her steward, "This is a judges nightmare, first is the Borzoi, but after that, I haven't got a clue"! I was over the moon, my first ever dog show and we won!

Of course, after that I thought showing was easy, I was soon to learn!

I learnt how to enter for Championship Shows. The first one we went to, there were only two in my class, I thought it would be a walk over, we were 2nd!

There was one other amusing incident; I took her to the Borzoi Club Champion Show, having entered her in the "Special Stud Dog or Brood Bitch" class. It was being judged by her original breeder, not the man I had bought her from. It was a well filled class, when it was my turn, the judge, who's favourite expression was "My Dear", said, "My dear, this is Bessie my dear, isn't it my dear?" I replied that it was and that I was afraid she was a little lame. "Oh my dear, if she is lame, my dear, you don't have to move her, my dear" nothing daunted, I set across the ring, doing my triangle and up and down, Bessie going, dot and carry, dot and carry, her arthritis was really bad that day. We came to line up for the final decision, she picked her winner, a beautiful black male, my thoughts were wandering, when she came up to me, "My dear, do concentrate my dear, I have just placed you second my dear, and therefore my dear, best brood bitch"!

The storm clouds were gathering again though, Bessie loved to swim, water was irresistible to her, every pond, every stream, it was her dream. One morning, as she came out of a pond, I noticed, where the wet feathering clung to her leg, a small lump on her stifle, it was very hard. I took her to my vet, who referred her to a veterinary clinic. My worst fears were confirmed, bone cancer. I felt sick with shock and horror. Then I was given a gamble of a chance. It was made very clear to me, that this was an experiment in its infancy and that so far, there had been no results from it. Bessie had to go to Addenbrooks, a big local hospital, where they would experiment on her, with a new anaesthetic and radiation. I agreed, I was clutching at straws.

"Can you go today?" she asked, I nodded numb. She made the 'phone call in front of me, only to be told they were full. "Oh come on, you can make room for one more, she's only tiny"! We went. When I got to the hospital, there in a special waiting room put aside for us, were about half a dozen dogs. Eventually, it was our turn. Bessie was laid on a trolley and given the anaesthetic; I had my arms around her. Within seconds, she was out cold. She was wheeled into the radiation room, I wasn't allowed to go with her, but I could watch what was going on, on a closed circuit television. For a very few seconds, an instrument beamed radiation on to the lump, a buzzer went off and immediately, she was wheeled back to me. In no time at all, she came round and we lifted her off the trolley on to the floor. She was steady enough to walk to the car and jump in without any help. That evening, as with every other evening after the treatment, she ate her dinner and showed no signs of distress.

She had five further sessions of this, any more and apparently, the bone would have shattered. After the final one, I prayed and prayed, knowing if it hadn't worked, I had reached the end of the line.

The day after her last treatment, feeling sick to the stomach, I took her back to the animal clinic … The bone had shrunk, the cancer was dead!! Sadly, not everyone was as lucky as we were. Some months after this, my vet asked me if I was prepared to give an interview to a national newspaper, on my success story. I was more than happy to oblige. When it was published, it was shattering, going on the lines, why should dogs have this treatment, when human beings were crying out for it. I just could not believe what I had read. This experiment had been done on dogs to see if it was safe for humans.

Bessie lived until she was nearly twelve, a good age, but not a great one. During her life, I learnt that she had been bred from many, many times, then she had the bone cancer and its treatment, all this must have taken a toll on her, but I like to think that the time she spent with me, were wonderful, happy years for her.

During her lifetime, she had an amazing talent for catching moles. We would be out walking and suddenly, without any warning, she would nosedive, fox like, into the ground and come up with a mole in her mouth. If for any reason, she failed to catch one, she would continue to burrow until she did! She must have caught hundreds that way, over the years.

One happy last memory of her, riding my horse over the neighbouring farmer's stubble fields, with Bessie, the whippet and Dana , (who I will come to next), in search of hares, the Pigmy goat that I had at the time, got loose and joined us. The Borzoi's had put up a hare and were going flat out, the whippet, not far behind them, suddenly, there the goat was, galloping with the best of them, I don't know what he thought he was chasing, but he had one hell of a gallop that day, and I nearly fell off my horse with laughter.

Darling Bessie, in some ways I think of you as my first Borzoi, your lovely daughter's life was cut so cruelly short.

For ever in my thoughts, my beloved Undomiel Blestka of Matalona.

Chapter 4, Dana's Story

After Bessie had been with me for a few months, I began to feel it would be nice for her, to have a companion, another Borzoi, not that it wouldn't be nice for me as well! I went to see the person who I had Bessie from and put this to him. The bitch I wanted was Anna, Bessie's mother, a pretty grey and white bitch. She was old yes, but I felt I could give her a good home for the last few years of her life, living in the house, being warm and dry.

The answer was a flat NO. "What would people say if I parted with an old bitch?" He did offer me Bessie's brother, who I would dearly have loved, but in those days, I thought having a male, with two bitches, was going to cause added problems, so reluctantly, I said no.

On my return home, as I said earlier, I had been thinking ahead.

I bought a weekly dog paper and poured over the Borzoi information for several weeks, until, at last! There it was what I had been searching for. A Borzoi breeder was advertising a litter of puppies.

I rang him immediately, I told him I had a strange request, I didn't want a puppy, but an older bitch as a companion for Bessie. Mike was shocked! He said he had never been asked that before. He took my number and said he would ring me back. For two days, I hung around the 'phone, grabbing it every time it rang, only to be disappointed. Then it happened! You can have Dana but, you will have to come here first and meet me and her and, in the long run, it is not what you want, it is not what I want, but what Dana wants.

I agreed and went north, to meet them. Michael's home and kennels were beautiful, I really enjoyed being there, infact, I made at least two more trips to see them, before I brought Dana home.

Sadly, we had a very shaky start. Dana claimed her place in the room and I put a comfortable bed there for her. She got along fine with Bessie and the whippet, that part was all OK, it was me she didn't like. She refused to leave her bed in the mornings and, when I went to put a lead on her, to take her for a walk, she bit me.

I tried and I tried, god knows how I tried and how many times she bit me. Eventually, I knew what I had to do. With a heavy heart, I 'phoned Mike and told him that I would bring her back to him.

Fate must have been on my side, for the next few weeks, Mike was unable to have her back. I didn't know whether to be happy for myself, or sad for Dana. Then the tide turned.

I was walking the three of them one morning, when the whippet put up a hare, she and Bessie set off after it, to my horror, Dana slipped her lead and tore off after them. They disappeared, out of sight, I was frantic. After twenty minutes or so, Bessie and Meg came back … No Dana. This is the end I thought, I will never see her again.

Then, just as I was thinking of going home to 'phone the police and the farmer, in the distance, I saw this black dog, heading towards home. Dana, I screamed and rushed towards her, the black dog broke into a canter and ran towards me … Yes, ran towards ME. She jumped up at me, putting her paws on my shoulders and licked my face. I held on to her tightly, crying my eyes out. The bond had been made between us, she never went back to Mike!

I do remember Mike coming to stay, to see Dana and how she lived; she gave him the same treatment, refused to speak to him, just lay on her bed and glared. Maybe, she had not forgiven him for giving her away, or maybe, she thought he had come to take her home. We will never know.

Around this period, my beloved Meg developed pyametra; my vet was unable to save her. I was devastated. She was the last of my whippets, I have never had another one, my mind is now totally focused on the Borzoi. May be one day, who knows, I am a sucker for a rescue!

Eventually, I began to think in terms of another dog, but as I have just said, there is only one breed for me … I rang Mike. This was not a good move, my husband, who basically was not a dog lover, hit the roof. Nothing daunted, I headed north again and came home with Nova! I never regretted it, but I did endure several weeks of not being spoken to. Not a happy situation.

Then came the move, we had been at Shelford for less than three years, when a house that my husband had always wanted, came on the market. We took a family vote on it, my husband, mother, two children and myself. I was the only one to vote no. Come to think of it, as I still wasn't being spoken to, so I suppose I was lucky to be included!

So we moved and twenty plus years on, this is where I am writing this from and, I love it.

The house needed a terrific amount doing to it and for well over a year, we lived with builders, their noise and their dust. Ugh!!!

I was really worried about the affect the move would have on the Zois, particularly Dana, I did not want her unsettled again. She took it in her stride, but she was a nightmare, she decided that all builders were there to be bitten, they hated her and she hated them!

One evening, we were in the kitchen having our supper, the dogs were in the sitting room, at the time, we still had no proper flooring on the passages, just hardboard, which certainly was uneven in parts. I heard one of the dogs walking on this, then to my horror, I heard a different sound, like someone with a hosepipe, I had no doubt as to what it was and the anger it would cause. Making an excuse to pass the open door, I saw Dana doing the biggest puddle ever; it seemed to go on forever too. I turned on the tap as fast as possible, to mask the noise, while I thought what to do next. I knew if my husband found out, there would be big, big, trouble.

As luck would have it, our downstairs lavatory was down the passage, behind the kitchen and past Dana's pee!

I remembered, there was an artificial cyclamen in the lavatory, "Just going to the loo" I said, forgetting to turn off the running tap. On my return, "The cyclamen in the lavatory is looking a little short of water, I must give it some, before I forget" I filled the jug from the still running tap, Dana had finished and returned to her bed and I turned the tap off, for the maximum noise that was to come. I clutched my jug, which was unbreakable and did an exaggerated trip on the hardboard floor, dropping the jug right over Dana's little accident! My husband never knew what she had done. Mike was to say to me later, I deserved an Oscar!!

Dana was quite at home here, but she tolerated no body outside the family.

One evening, we had a friend for supper, with his two teenage sons. Both boys needed the loo on separate occasions. Dana lay in wait and had them both, grabbing a leg. I am ashamed to say, we all, including their father, thought this rather funny. Now that I am older and wiser, I do not find it amusing.

Dana was a thief, then what Borzoi isn't? This one though, was one to end all others. It was our first Christmas here and we were many for lunch. On Christmas Eve, I had prepared a great mountain of Brussels Sprouts, ready to cook the next day. On my return to the kitchen, later that evening, there was Dana, head in the sprout bowl and just two left! Raw sprouts? Why she didn't blow, I will never know.

Dana's end was terrible, it was in the winter of 1986, on Boxing Day, she was only 9 years old. I woke to a pouring wet day; it had rained all that Christmas day and presumably, all the night. I put my three girls on their leads and walked them up to the neighbouring park, where I let them loose, as I had done many times before. There was a small stream to cross, never a problem, for them or for me. It was about 6am and pitch dark. When I got to the stream, I could see it was very swollen, much wider than it had ever been, the water was running hard. Bessie and Nova jumped over it effortlessly, I knew it was too wide and deep for me. I turned to Dana, who was at my side and I started to say, Darling, this is too much for us. In the middle of the sentence, she took off, in the dim light, I saw her fall into the water, just crumble, I jumped in, it was up to my waist, grabbed her head, to keep it above water. I am pretty certain she was already dead. Try as I might, I did not have enough strength to pull her out.

How very lucky I was, that the farmer had come to feed his cattle that were in the field, at this time of the morning. He had heard my screams and came to help. Together, we pulled Dana on to the bank, but she was dead, dead, dead. Kindly, he put the body and Bessie and Nova into his truck and drove us all home.

Sleep tight my beloved girl,

"There comes a mist and a blinding rain

And life is never the same again".

How true in your case, my beloved.

Chapter 5 – Nova's Story

As I said, Nova came to me after the death of my lovely Meg. She settled in without any trouble, an easier, quieter, gentler dog, you could not wish for. Luckily for her, I am sure she was unaware of the icy atmosphere that surrounded her arrival.

She took the move to here, without any problems and unlike her cousin Dana, had no problem with the builders, although it did amuse me, they looked quite alike, and the builders certainly couldn't tell the difference!

After we had sorted ourselves out in our new home, I thought it would be nice to show her. So, with Mike's help and guidance, we started going to shows. This again, was not a popular move with husband, especially if the show was on a weekend, which they normally were, he liked me here, to look after him and the family.

Nova though, didn't really enjoy it, it just wasn't her scene, but she was giving me a taste of the years to come.

One show, the Borzoi Club Centenary Championship show in 1992, sticks out in my mind. We had all been asked to dress as they would have done, in 1892. I went to the local "Hire a costume" shop and was thrilled with what I hired, a beautiful full length black velvet dress, complete with hooped petticoat and muff. I thought I looked really glamorous and thought it would look so good beside my beautiful black girl! Well, what does one do with a muff when you are showing a dog? It soon got discarded! But, there was worse to come, the hooped petticoat stuck out so much, that Nova was yards from me, then I tried to run and the damn thing swung around like a demented top, banging into poor Nova, she was not amused.

As we made our wobbly way round the ringside, Mike, who was standing watching the class, said in a loud voice, meant for me to hear, "Which of those two, is the self black bitch do you suppose?" That finished me, I gave way to hysterical laughter, needless to say, and we didn't get placed!

The nearest we ever got to winning, was with our local newspaper, The Echo, who ran a competition to find the most appealing local dog. I entered Nova and took her along to their photographic studios, where they photographed her, lying on some ghastly fake fur rug, with a bunch of plastic leaves in the background! The day the pictures were printed, to find the winner of the competition, I bought as many Echo's as I could afford and voted for her, encouraging everyone I knew, to do the same. Nova was second, beaten by a ball of fluff, with big eyes. However, we were presented with a framed photograph!

Nova lived a quiet unassuming life; she was a joy, never any trouble, loving, gentle, a delight. She died on 1995, a month before her twelfth birthday.

Chapter 6, Vodka's story.

As I have said, Nova gave me the taste for showing; I was beginning to meet people, having fun and enjoying myself. Realising that Nova was not happy in the ring, I decided to brave my husband's wrath yet again, and buy myself a possible show bitch. This time, I wanted a puppy. I made some enquiries and was told of a nice litter that I went to see, this is what I saw.

It was wonderful, for the first time, I could name my own Borzoi!

Remembering my mother's thoughts on Bubbly, I had no option than to name her Vodka. I rang the breeder, to tell her this, "Oh dear", she said, "this is my "L" litter, Oh, simple! Longuin Lemon Vodka".

What fun she was and how lovely to have a puppy in the house again. Dear Nova, took her in her stride, as usual, even my husband was better about her than I expected! I could fill these pages with pictures of her puppy hood, magical dream days.

Eventually, her show career began and, joy of joys, she enjoyed it.

I did too, but sadly, we were both novices and I had an awful lot to learn, I have to be honest, I never gave her a chance, I was her handicap. People were kind, explained my faults and mistakes and I was as happy as a sand boy. Getting the odd reserve and VHC, was as good to me, as winning at Crufts! We did get to Crufts though, by getting a second, in the Borzoi Championship Show, in 1990.

At this point, I cannot lie; she was handled by someone else!

I can still laugh at one occasion at Leeds Ch. It was an incredibly hot day and although I was under a shady tree, she began to feel the heat badly. I took a towel out of my bag and soaked it under a cold tap, then put it over her, to try and cool her down. I was sitting beside Mike at the time, when I realised it was nearly time for my class. I got her up and took the towel off her. Then I realised what I had done, the towel was bright red and the colour had run all over her. "Talk about Longuin Lemon Vodka, more like, Longuin Bloody Mary!" Another of Mike's classics! We never made the ring! But, Oh! How we laughed!

Another amusing incident with Vodka; I had some borzoi friends

Staying, we were preparing to sit down to a meal, Vodka was lying on the bench beside the table, taking up rather a lot of room. One of my friends tried to push her away, to make room for him to sit down, she refused to budge, feeling irritated, he said to her, "Vodka, you are just about the ugliest Borzoi I have ever seen." She gave him a baleful look and without any effort or warning, opened her mouth and was sick all over his lap!

She was such a gifted intelligent girl. On my way home from a show, she would sleep soundly in the back of the car, until we got to within about one mile from home, when she would wake immediately and stand up, her tail wagging, it was always the same place, how did she know?

Vodka died in 1998 aged ? She began to have trouble with her breathing, which slowly grew worse. The dreadful day I took her to the vet, I had no idea of the seriousness and sorrow, that day would bring. She was X-rayed and it showed her heart had become drastically enlarged, it was making it impossible for her to breath, eventually and not too far ahead, she would suffocate. I had no choice. My vet offered to put her to sleep then and there, or bring her round, so that I could take her home and come out later to do it. All these years later, I think I made the wrong decision, I brought her home … What a dreadful day it was.

Once, at the ringside, I was overheard by one of our most respected Borzoi breeders, describing her as the "Perfect Borzoi", he laughed and didn't quite agree with me. Sorry Reg, this time you were wrong, but then, love is blind.

Chapter 7 - Oprah's Story

If I had been keen on showing with Nova, it was nothing compared to the fun I had with Vodka. Suddenly, I became ambitious, no longer content with the odd VHC, I wanted to win!

Behind my husband's back, I spoke to one really good Borzoi friend that I have, about my feelings. She told me of this superb litter that had been born, that the breeder was keeping a bitch for herself, but she was prepared to have a word with her and see if she would be prepared to change her mind and let me have her. I was amazed; I had heard how wonderful this litter was. My heart was in my mouth!

A few days later, my friend 'phoned, with this breeder's telephone number. "She would like you to ring her", she said. I waited for my husband to go out; I knew this would be certain trouble! I remember that day; he seemed to hang around forever.

Eventually, I was alone and on that telephone. "I think I know you", she said sharply to me. "You have a black Nakora bitch that Mike occasionally shows for you, if I let you have this puppy, at times I would like to show her". I agreed … After a lot more questions, Oprah was mine. Needless to say, my husband was NOT amused; I would not be exaggerating, if I said he was furious.

What a beautiful girl she was, what a beautiful head.

As soon as she was six months, she entered her first puppy class at Championship level, there were a lot in that class, which she won, handled by her breeder. A few weeks later, another puppy class, again she won, this time handled by me, I was over the moon, my first, first, I was on the road to success!

It was a ding dong battle with her litter sister, sometimes it was my day and, sometimes it was Odette's day, occasionally, it was Odell's day, another litter sister. There was also a winning male, Orlando, what a litter.

Oprah, Vodka and Nova, were firm friends. I continued to show Vodka along with Oprah, while Nova rested on her laurels.

Sadly, in 1991, my poor husband developed cancer. He went through devastating sessions of chemotherapy, to no avail, he died early in 1993. I will never forget the last few days before he died. He was gravely ill upstairs in bed, we knew the end was near, when Vodka and Oprah started behaving oddly, they both kept asking to be let out, once outside, they would stand under the bedroom window and howl like a couple of Banshees, it was dreadful, they must have known.

About a couple of weeks after his death, I woke one morning and realised I was suppose to have taken them both to a local Hound Show. I didn't feel like going, but, I argued with myself, what are you going to do all day, here on your own? It was less than an hour's drive, so I put two unwashed dogs in the car and set off for the show.

Oprah won her class, which as far as I can remember, was Limit and we then went in for Best of Breed, which to my utter amazement, she won … … … I was in shock!! I began to pack up and prepare to go home. "Where do you think you are going?" said a Borzoi friend of mine. "Home" I said, "I just need to go home". "What on earth for, you have nothing to go home for now and, it is an insult to your judge not to stay for Best in Show", this pulled me up sharp, she's right, I thought to myself so I stayed. It was a long drawn out day, as BIS, was not until late afternoon, when all judging had finished, twenty seven breeds in all.

At last the moment arrived, we were called in, in alphabetical order, i.e. Afghan's first, when the compare called out, "Next is the winning Borzoi, Yadasar Oprah, who beat twenty three Borzoi's to be here", I felt so proud, but I did have a lump in my throat!

After the judge had looked at all the dogs and made them all move round the very large ring, she selected ten, for her final choice. I couldn't believe it, Oprah was one! At this point, I glanced up at the spectator's gallery and saw my friend who had shocked me into staying; I felt joy that she was still there.

Again, she went over her remaining dogs and again, she sent us round the ring. I had barely pulled up and, certainly hadn't stood Oppie properly, when she marched over to me and shook my hand. I had won BEST IN SHOW!

What a day, and to think I nearly didn't go, or stay for BIS, I have a lot to thank that friend for.

Eventually, I got used to living here on my own. I made one alteration, I took Vodka and Oprah upstairs to sleep, not Nova, she always hated stairs. It was the empty bedroom I hated most and they certainly helped.

Life went on and so did my showing, Oprah was winning, or getting well placed. Our first setback, came when I took her to North Wales, for their Champion show. It was being judged by one of our most respected judges, at that time, the only judge to have been passed to judge every breed. I had a bit of a crush on him too, like many others. Oprah won her class under him, Post Graduate, I think it was and went into the line up for the Bitch C.C. something upset her, she got in a real mood, just refused to move. Four times he asked me to try again, but no, she just wouldn't budge. I feel sure, if this hadn't happened, she would have had the C.C. that day. Oh well! You take the rough with the smooth.

The smooth was just round the corner! In May 1995, I took the girls to the Scottish Championship show, full of high hopes that were soon to be dashed, when I found the Crufts Borzoi and Hound Group winner, in my class. I was so disappointed, no way, was I going to beat her. But, I DID! I must have had a very brave judge. Oprah got her first C.C. I cannot remember now how many R.C.C.'s she had, it was something in the region of ten, the first of which she got at Paington, out of Junior!

The following year, during which she collected a good many of those R.C.C.'s, I returned to Scotland under the same judge who had tried so hard for her in Wales. She won it, Open Bitch and we went in for the C.C. He judged all his winners again and on walking back to the table, to pick

up the Challenge Certificate, he came past me at close range, "You have nothing to worry about", he said without even looking at me.

Oprah had one more to go, before she gained her Crown! It happened only seven days later, from a most unlikely source.

We went to Bath, under a breed specialist. I sat with a friend and commented, "If I put Oppie in a bath of black die, I would have a chance". The judge preferred black Borzoi's! But we won. In the challenge, it ended between Oprah and Odette. "I am going to make you two work for this", she said and, she did! Then the heart fluttering moment, when she goes to the table, to pick up the C.C. You stand and pray! She walked straight to me! I was the proud owner of Champion Yadasar Oprah … My showing dream had come true; I had made up my first Champion.

The anxious wait, look at her, she is beautiful.

The magic moment.

I think this says it all!

Oprah never gained another C.C. shades of the Welsh Kennel Club show, were beginning to appear, she was not enjoying showing, although, she did win Veteran classes at Borzoi shows, as well as many great awards during her life time, including Best of Breed in the Borzoi open show, in 1996 and reserve best of breed, at the champion show, the year before.

Oprah left me, at the age of 10. She was old by now and I was aware that she had dangerous lumps in her mammary glands, but I also knew that an operation, at this stage, was not a consideration. I was so lucky, until the final day, she showed no signs of distress, she ate she walked, just slept a lot. That morning, I knew it was bad; she didn't even want to look at me. I called my vet, my wonderful first champion, died in my arms. I am just sad, that my husband, who always scoffed at my showing dogs, did not live to see me make up my first Champion.

God bless you Oppie, where ever you are, we will meet, with all the others, at the Rainbow Bridge.

"Brothers and sisters I bid you beware

Never give your heart to a dog to tare."

Chapter 8, The "Duckworth Delinquents" Their Stories

Skye **Blue** **Mouse**

As I said, my husband died in 1993, my immediate reaction, was to get another Borzoi, but I did realise that I might not be thinking straight, too much emotion and all that! So I promised myself, no more dogs for six months. This in hindsight was good reasoning. Today, I have memories of dangerous thoughts, like having one of every large hound breed, not a good idea! So thankfully, I waited.

Around this time, I had been captivated by an American import, Ch. Virginia Reel, who had arrived in this country, in whelp. Her importer swiftly made her a UK Champion; she was a truly beautiful bitch. After my self imposed six months were up, I decided that this is where I was going to go. I wanted a self black bitch. By now, I knew the breeder concerned quite well, he knew what I wanted, so one day, I went down to Devon, where he lived, to see his litter of grandchildren from Virginia Reel.

Sitting in his house, soon after my arrival, he came in with a beautiful black bitch puppy in his arms. This was to be Skye, my first Virginia grand daughter. The following morning, I asked him if I could have another puppy from the litter, as I felt they would be company for one another. He agreed, and we went out to have a look at the babies, for me to choose another one. Well, I never chose one, he chose me. One blue and white male, persistently crawled out from the litter and made his way on to my lap, as fast as I returned him to the rest, he disentangled himself and came back to me … … What choice did I have? I needed a male, with all my bitches, like a hole in the head!

Early in January 1994, my Devon breeder telephoned and said it was time for me to have the puppies and that he would bring them up to me. "By the way" he said, "I am not sure now, whether I made the right choice for you, over the black bitch, she does look as though she is going to be a very big bitch. I have another self black, from a later litter, which you have not seen, I think she is nicer, so I will bring her up as well and you can make your choice." How excited I was! The three youngsters arrived, late one afternoon on the 15th January. We piled the three of them, all together on a large bed in my utility room, where they settled in, without any problems, presumably, they were pretty tired from their long journey.

It was decision time, I think, even before they arrived, I knew what I was going to do! My daughter clinched it for me. "Oh Mummy!" she said, looking at the new option, who, being from a later litter, was smaller than the other two. "You must have that one, she looks just like a little mouse"!

So, Skye, Blue and Mouse, came to live with Nova, Vodka and Oprah!

I think the breeder, was somewhat worried about not taking one home. When he left, the next morning, he asked me to 'phone his wife to say he was on his way home, and to tell her, he was coming back with an empty car. He said words to the affect, that he would rather I told her than him!

When the rest of the Borzoi world, heard I had bought three pups from him, they were somewhat surprised to say the least, so to keep them quiet, we concocted this story. "Well, you see, he was having a sale, buy two and get one free"! It was amazing how many of them believed this tale!

At the time of their arrival, they were about eight weeks old. Now, it was time to think of names. Mouse was easy, what else could I have called her! The other two, I had to think about. My late husband was not a dog lover, but, I felt I needed to, in some ways, include him. He was a Highlander, from Kyle of Lochalsh, where the ferry used to go from, to the Isle of Skye. I wanted to call the original choice, Skye Boat Song, he loved that song. Sadly, Boat Song was a whippet prefix and, unallowed by the Kennel Club, but the very kind secretary phoned me and suggested Song of Skye, she became Sholwood Song of Skye of Russkaya. My next problem was my beautiful boy. Up near Kyle, there is a beautiful stretch of water, known as, The Sound of Sleet, I wanted that, their breeder was horrified, sounds like "Sound asleep" he said, so I had to think again. My husband had often, very tunelessly, whistled, "I Never Felt More Like Singing the Blues", this was my option, he became Sholwood Singing the Blues of Russkaya, The others accepted them, without any problems and peace reigned, but not for long!!

They reached their early teens and, like all teenagers, they went wild! They had reached the age of destruction!

Skye and Blue, chose to sleep together, in a little porch between the utility room door and the back door and Mouse, in the utility room, so sleeping arrangements were easy. The back door opened onto a small, courtyard, which had a door leading into a walled garden, so they had plenty of room to run around in, from which they could not get out of. As I said, they had become teenagers and they set out on a trail of vandalism. Within a very few weeks, they had destroyed the garden, they dug holes everywhere, pinching anything from the house, that they could get hold of and buried it in the garden. I lost count on the amount of reading glasses, gloves, shoes, etc. I found buried there. I am afraid it made me laugh, but some of my visitors, didn't find it so funny. A girlfriend came to stay, who was a very keen needle woman, she was working on a beautiful tapestry, which she had very nearly finished. I did warn her, but … … she left the tapestry on the chair, where she had been sitting, in the sitting room, while she went upstairs, only for a minute, but it was long enough, when she came down, it was gone. I knew where to look! There it was, in pieces, each piece carefully buried. Well! I had warned her.

The utility room, was a room I was rather proud of, I had "papered" it with all my prize cards, from Oprah's many firsts, and seconds, down to VHC. I had so many, the walls were completely covered, it looked really affective. Slowly they began to disappear, scattered over the walled garden. I gave up; it kept them amused for hours! Then I noticed the really high ones were being removed, this really puzzled me, I had put them up with the help of a step ladder. I hid and watched. Mouse came charging in from the garden, reached the top of three small steps that led into the utility room and took off, she reached an incredible height and, another prize card hit the dust!

Eventually, the time arrived for them to make their show debut, the show was Southern Counties, under a Finnish judge, Vodka and Oprah came as well, I had a friend with me and we went in two cars. No one from the Borzoi world had seen the "Delinquents", which made it all the more amusing. Blue was entered in Puppy Dog, so he was the first to make his appearance, not many in the class, but he won it. Then the long wait for the Bitch classes, Mouse, in Minor Puppy, went first … She won. The following class, Puppy, saw Skye. "Oh zee buutiful bitch" says my judge, "lets see if she does zee move as buutiful" She did, she won! By this time, it was getting increasingly funny, watching the look on other peoples faces but, we hadn't finished yet! Limit Bitch and it was Oprah's turn … She won, just a slight set back in the next class, Open Bitch with Vodka, she wasn't placed!

So we come to Best Puppy and I had to find two handlers, for Blue and Mouse. Remembering the judged comments on Skye, I decided to handle her myself. Best puppy was proclaimed, Blue, served me right! This qualified Blue for Best puppy in the Hound Group. This was won by an Irish Wolfhound, I thought that was me finished, that the judge wouldn't choose another large dog, she would pick one of the small hound winners … She chose Blue. My greatest day out!!

Mouse　　　　Skye　　　　Blue　　　　Oprah

The following March, as they had all qualified, we went to Crufts and, what a Crufts it was! It had been my dream since I started showing, to have a first at that show.
They were all out of puppy by now, and Mouse and Blue were in Yearling. Blue, being the male, was in the ring first. He was a very strong dog and I was finding him difficult to handle, so I asked his breeder to take him in the ring for me. He wasn't very keen on doing so, as he had a dog in a later class but, he had an Australian Borzoi breeder staying with him and, he offered to take him for me.
It was a big class and Milan handled the dog beautifully, winning it. My excitement knew no bounds, my first, first at Crufts.

Then the long wait for the bitches and Mouse's turn. Again, an extremely well filled class. I felt sick, my hands shook, I was literally shaking with nerves. Once in the ring, it looked enormous and, certainly felt it, as we made our way round it. At last, it was all over and we all stood our dogs, waiting for our judges' decision. I felt faint, she was pointing towards me. I must have got it wrong, she must mean left or right of me but, she didn't,
I had won my second, first, but this time, handled by me!!!

Things continued on a high for me too that day, Skye, in the following class gained a third and Oprah in the top class, Open bitch, a second. I don't suppose I will ever have such a wonderful Crufts again!!

Chapter 9, Mouse's story.

As I have already said, Mouse was the unplanned addition to the new family, an addition I will never regret. She was an absolute delight in every way. By far the naughtiest of the three and, I am certain, a dreadful gossip, sticking her nose into the others faces and, dancing round them barking, trying to encourage them to get up to mischief. Not a difficult task!

Her showing career had a very promising start, in the following September after her Crufts success, she put her feet on the first rung of the ladder towards her crown, by being awarded the R.C.C. from Junior, at Darlington, in 1995. I was amazed and overjoyed! She continued a successful run, consistently winning, or being placed and in 1998, gained her first C.C. in Scotland, a wonderful moment! We stayed overnight in Edinburgh, for that show. I managed to find a dog friendly hotel and, upon being shown to our room, was amazed to find she had been given her own bed, a couple of cuddly toys and a bowl of water. It certainly was a "dog friendly" place but … None of these were suitable for anything larger than a Yorkshire Terrier! Soon after this, tragedy struck!

We were exercising the dogs, early one morning, giving them free running. Mouse chased a rabbit and disappeared out of sight but, not out of sound. We heard the most terrible screams coming from her. Upon getting to her, I found she could not put her left hind leg to the ground. Her cries were terrible. We managed to get her into the car and took her to the vets, where the news was bad. She had torn her cruciate ligament; this was to need special and complicated surgery. My vet was not prepared to do this and referred me to a practice that specialised in this, about an hours drive away. We were able to go immediately, when we arrived, having signed the consent form, I met the surgeon who was going to perform the operation, a more surly man I have yet to meet. I am always in a state, when anything is wrong with my dogs and in particular, when an anaesthetic is necessary.

For something to say, I remarked words to the affect that it would happen to my best Show bitch. "How old is she?" he enquired. "Nearly five", I said.

"You show people are all the same, you only think of the shows, not your dogs. I would have thought at this age, you would have had the best out of her. One thing I will tell you, you will never show her again. After this, she will never be sound again." I was shattered and so upset that he had read my feelings for my dogs so wrongly. I left her there in tears and in shock at his cruel words.

She came through the operation successfully and I was allowed to fetch her home the next day. The nurse explained the operation to me, when I fetched her, so I was spared seeing the man again. It was a long and slow progress. She could not put her leg to the ground to start with and, she looked so strange, with that back leg completely shaved. Eventually, she began to put a little pressure on it and I began to take her for short, slow walks. After a time, I began to increase this, ten minutes, twenty and so on. Then I struck luck, a friend of mine, who lived a couple of miles away, had a dog walker that she was prepared to let me use. Every day, I would put her in the car and take her there. Like the walking, I slowly increased the time and speed on the walker. The next move was to get someone to drive me up there and, after the session, I would walk her home. Then we got to the stage when I was walking her there and back, wonderful!!!

Her shaved leg and feathering grew back and I was convinced she was sound. I decided it was time to show again. A little over one year later from the accident, I took her to Birmingham; there she won her second C.C. I'm afraid I bust into tears. My poor judge was totally shocked by my reaction, until I told her the story, then she cried with me!

A few weeks later, I read my "write up", in the dog papers. Her critique was glowing, but the bit I loved the best, was her comment about her marvellous movement and wonderful drive from behind! I photocopied it and sent it to that surgeon; he never even had the manners to acknowledge it!

Mouse had one final rung to climb, that came in the September of that year, at the City of Birmingham, where she received, not only the Bitch C.C. but also, B.O.B. I had my second Champion!

Between the two Birmingham shows, she also got Reserve Best in Show, at our local Open Show, under that famous All Rounder, that had tried so hard with Oprah, all those years before.

She received her last R.C.C. from Veterans, at the Hound Show, in 2002, under Milan, the Australian, who had handled Blue for me, in their yearling days at Crufts. This is another story and, all though it is Mouse's, it is better put in Blue's Story.

She ended her career, with a Best Veteran at both the Borzoi Club show and the Northern Borzoi and finally, at Crufts, seven years after her first win there, in 2003.

Mouse died toward the end of 2005, the last of the delinquents to leave me.

Chapter 10 - Skye's Story.

Looking at her picture now, it seems an age ago, since that fluffy little bundle was placed in my arms, when I was choosing my self black bitch.

In hindsight, her breeder was right, she was a very big bitch, quite a masculine girl but, oh so striking, and spectacular in the ring, she just loved it. She would move and stand herself perfectly; she needed no handling at all. In the line up, she would stand motionless, with her gaze fixed firmly on the judge, as if to say, "Don't you dare not place me first"!

She had a real presence about her.

Because of her size and masculinity, I had to pick my judges carefully; I knew not many would like her type. Then later, when Mouse was doing so well, I found I was concentrating more on her than Skye but, we did have our moments.

In the May of 1995, I was going to the Scottish show with Oprah and Vodka and Skye's breeder asked me if I could bring a bitch home for him. A litter sister to Skye and Blue, needed re-homing from Scotland. I agreed and arrangements were made for me to pick Petra up from the show ground.

Not a very pleasant experience, partly because the lady who handed her over to me, was crying her eyes out, I never asked why she was sending her back, and partly because I was none too sure how Oprah and Vodka would behave, with a strange bitch in the car on a six hour drive back home. That I need not have worried about, you would have thought they had known each other all their lives.

I had been asked if I would keep the bitch for a few days until he was able to collect her, or found a home for her. A few days went into weeks. Petra settled in, slept in the house, became a firm member of the family and, I fell in love. By early June, I rang and said I would like to keep her. Things moved fast from that moment. The answer was a definite NO; he wanted her back for breeding. I remembered the Bessie incident and tried to make the same arrangements, but no, he just got angry. On the 16th of June, he 'phoned early in the morning, to say he was coming to get her and, by middle afternoon, in floods of tears, he took her away from me. I will never, ever forget Petra. I did ask if I could have her back, when he had finished with her, but he never did. The incident had other sad implications too, we had been such good friends, now, we do not speak, other than a stiff good morning or hello.

However, to return to Skye, I took her, Mouse and Blue to Bournemouth, in the August of that year. To my horror, he was there with Petra. The poor bitch had never forgotten me; the look in her eyes told me that. I found the whole experience devastating.

Our judge that day was a whippet person and, I felt he would prefer Mouse, as she was so much finer than Skye. I was wrong there, Mouse, I think was third but Skye, in the next class, Limit Bitch, won it, I was delighted. Then came Open Bitch, with Petra, who won. My heart was in my mouth, I would have to stand next to her for the challenge. Then I got the shock of my life, the Bitch C.C. was awarded to … … Skye! One person, who must have known the story, came up and gave me a hug and said, "Darling, this is probably the best C.C. you will ever have"! Maybe it was, but to this day, I would have swapped it for Petra.

Skye was a compete couch potato, literally, that was the one seat in the living room that she claimed for herself.

As she grew older, she became very arthritic, her poor front toes became very deformed. Certain medicines did help her, but she began to want exercise less and less, which in its turn, caused a weight problem. Always a greedy bitch, this was a problem, until my vet put her on a diet food. Poor old girl, she didn't enjoy that too much, but it did do the trick, she became quite slim line again.

Her end was a terrible shock to me. That morning, she wanted to come on the first walk she had been on for ages, she was still pretty lame, so the girlfriend I had staying with me and I went on a reasonably long walk, but very slowly for her. She seemed to really enjoy it, came back and had her breakfast, then took up her usual position on the couch.

Pam and I played on my computer, seeing what we could buy, Borzoi wise on e-Bay. Time flew past and I went to the kitchen, to do some potatoes for lunch. To my utter horror, Skye was lying on the floor in the utility room, almost unconscious. I had never even heard her go through there. When my vet arrived, there was only one thing left to do; I don't think she even knew the vet was there. The first of my beloved "Delinquents" had left me.

"Speed bonny boat like a bird on the wing, over the sea to Skye".

Chapter 11, Blue's Story.

Blue, my precious boy, the dog that chose me, not me him, that was the best choice ever made. He was my gentle giant, my King of Hearts.

He was an outstandingly beautiful dog, starting his show career, as I have already said, by winning Best Puppy and reserve Best Puppy, in the Hound Group on his first appearance, in 1994. In 1995, he had eight firsts at Championship level. One judge's critique reads: "A white and blue 22 months, showing incredible maturity. Nice head, good forechest, and what I can call a textbook front having width and upper arm and shoulder of highest quality – a most lovely dog." I don't feel you can get better than that! He had a great many R.C.C's, his best being at Crufts in 1998, but never made the big one. There was at that time, a wonderful winning dog, Blue was always behind him, including the Crufts award. That's the way the luck goes, or as the Cookie Crumbles, as some would say!

As a house dog and my beloved pet, he was wonderful, but … he did have one little fault, what a thief! Being so tall, he could easily reach any part of the working top in my kitchen. One day, I had a friend coming for supper. I had taken two steaks out of the freezer and left the kitchen for less than a minute, one steak was missing! Blue was lying on a chair, with a large steak in his mouth, literally drooling. To this day, I can still see the saliva dripping from his mouth! I hadn't another steak, so there was nothing for it, but to grab it back, wash it and eat it myself. I am still here to tell the tale!

Another incident that comes to mind, I had been given some grouse, so I asked some friends round to help me eat them. You would have thought I would have learnt my lesson, but no, I left for a second, to get a roasting tin for them, when I returned, I was one grouse short. Blue though, had learnt his lesson, he took the bird outside on to the lawn. By the time I found him, it was in pieces and covered in grass from a newly mown lawn! Again, no option. I picked up the pieces, took them inside and washed the grass off. Obviously, that one had to be mine. When my guests arrived and we sat down to eat, one of them said, I can't manage grouse, I can't cut them up.

I am sure you can guess what I did!! … My whole one was delicious!

Slowly, the seeds of a thought began to grow in my head. An idea, that was to leave me devastated. By this time, through the internet, I had made contact with the breeder of Virginia Reel, the Delinquents grandmother. I was new to the computer and, so excited when I found his website! I e-mailed him, attaching a photograph of Mouse, telling him who she was. He got my picture but not my explanatory e-mail. It was not long before I had a reply. "Who is she? What is she? She's to die for"! We became friends over the internet and I told him about my thoughts, to have a litter from Mouse by Blue. I was concerned as I felt they might have been too closely related. His answer was, "Not close enough". It turned out that they would be having a litter around that time and we vaguely discussed a puppy exchange. An idea I really liked the sound of. I decided to go ahead with my idea.

I shall never forget that fateful day. A close friend and Borzoi breeder, lived a short distance from me. Never having done a mating, she agreed to come and give me some help. Blue and Mouse were together, but Blue was not showing an interest, although Mouse certainly was! She arrived and without any hesitation grabbed Blue by his penis and masturbated him. I have to say, I was shocked. It was to no avail and she promised to return later on in the day. When she did, we took them out into the courtyard, she knelt down to repeat her actions, Blue turned on her and bit her in the face. It was too awful and so much blood. Her husband came to collect her and our friendship was finished for life.

Any thoughts of my litter were over. I took Blue up to the local kennels, where I used to send him, when my bitches were in season. I can't remember ever being so gutted but, there was worse to come. I telephoned her the next morning, to see how she was and to again apologise. It was a horrible conversation, ending with her saying, she would not rest until my dog was put down. For this achievement, she reported me to the police, who passed it to the Crown Prosecution.

In a panic and foolishly, I turned to Blue's breeder for help. All I got there was a sharp letter, advising me to have the dog put down.

A few days after I had left Blue at the kennels, the owner telephoned me, asking me to take him to my vet, as there was a great deal of blood in his urine. I was just leaving the house to go to a funeral, so she called her own vet to him. The outcome of this and several further visits was suspected cancer of the prostrate. He was referred to a top specialist in Cambridge, who operated on him, removing his testicles and other cancerous tissue. He told me he never could have mated a bitch in his condition and, to have touched his penis, would have been agony for him. When I collected him, to bring him home, the nurse said, the surgeon had left a message for me. "My dog was a perfect gentleman." It brought tears to my eyes, I had never told the surgeon about what had happened.

Blue's life was saved, before the operation, the Crown Prosecution discarded the case. She took a private prosecution out on me, which was extremely unpleasant but I knew my dog was safe.

I felt so sick and upset with what had happened that I gave up showing. I knew she had told the whole of the Borzoi world, both here and abroad, what had happened and that I knew my dog was savage, I just couldn't face anyone. I was devastated. Then, I began to get telephone calls, in support, from people I hardly knew and cards and letters started to arrive, one or two people even came to see me, but it was at the Hound Show at Stafford before I showed again. I went, for two reasons, The Australian, who had handled Blue to victory at his first Crufts, had come over to judge the Borzoi and my good friend, who had managed to get the breeder to sell me Oprah, was treasurer of this show and had asked me to lunch afterwards, with the judges, a real honour. I felt sick to the stomach, on the journey there, on arrival, I could not believe the welcome I got, even some I could not put names to, came and gave me a hug, saying welcome back. The relief was immense! Of course, she was there, but there were enough people there for us to keep away from each other.

I said earlier, this should be in Mouse's story, for, it was Mouse that I took, entered in Veteran Bitch … She won and ended up by winning the R.C.C.! A wonderful comeback.

My beloved Blue, survived his operation well. He lived until the summer of 2005. His end, like his sister Skye, was thank God quick. One morning he seemed not quite himself, by the following morning, he was suffering badly. I called my vet, now the one who had helped and stood by him, during his troubles, I put my arms round him and we did what we had to do.

Goodbye my gentle giant, a perfect gentleman to the end.

I never felt more like Singing the Blues

Chapter 12, William's Story.

About the time of the Delinquents arrival, I received a 'phone call from Dubai, from my friend Carol, who was having a terrible struggle, rescuing hundreds of unwanted dogs that abounded in that country. I had said, if there was a Borzoi, let me know and I would do what I could to help. This call was about just that.

William's Tail, Told to Wag.

The following is what I wrote, after his death, about his story.
William was born in the Ukraine, probably in 1993. He was sent to Dubai by his breeder and placed in a pet shop, which was owned by the then, only vet in Dubai. My personal feelings are, vets should not own pet shops. Also Dubai is not a suitable country for a Borzoi, being a Russian breed, they cannot tolerate heat.
William was in the pet shop for a week before he was sold. I week after that, he was picked up by a main road, with two broken front legs. At the time, it was believed he was not more than 7 weeks old. He was taken to Carol, who ran the rescue in Dubai, but because of his legs, she had no alternative but to take him to the vet.
The vet operated on his legs but refused to let Carol have him. Instead, she loaned him to Terry and Sheila, telling them they were to return him to her as soon as the legs had recovered, as he

was to go back to her pet shop. Terry was at the time, stationed in the R.A.F. in Dubai. After a few weeks, Terry was ordered back to the UK and unbeknown to anyone except Sheila and Carol, he was put on a British Airways flight and flown to London. He then had to endure 6 months quarantine, not a pleasant thought for such a big and young dog, but infinitely better than going back into that pet shop.

At this point, Carol 'phoned me and asked me if I would place him in the Borzoi rescue, which I agreed to do, but I think I already knew what I was going to do! Terry sadly could not keep him, as he was permanently being stationed in different countries.

I went to visit him once a month. I would like to have gone more often but it was a four and a half hour journey from here to the quarantine kennels. After six long months, I made the journey for the last time. I can still remember my excitement getting there and the joy of seeing him jump into the back of my car, settling down straight away, as though he knew he was going home. Actually, it was not without a little concern, I had 5 Borzoi at home already, three of which were roughly the same age as William, teenagers I suppose and they certainly behaved like them!

Taking him away was a strange experience, I never expected to have tears from half the kennel staff, two girls begged me to let them keep him. I had given Terry my word I would have him and anyhow I wanted him! I think it goes to show what a wonderful character he had.

I owned this dog for a little over ten wonderful years, he was the most loving friend and he has left a gap in my life that can never be filled.

William, my "Joker Wills"

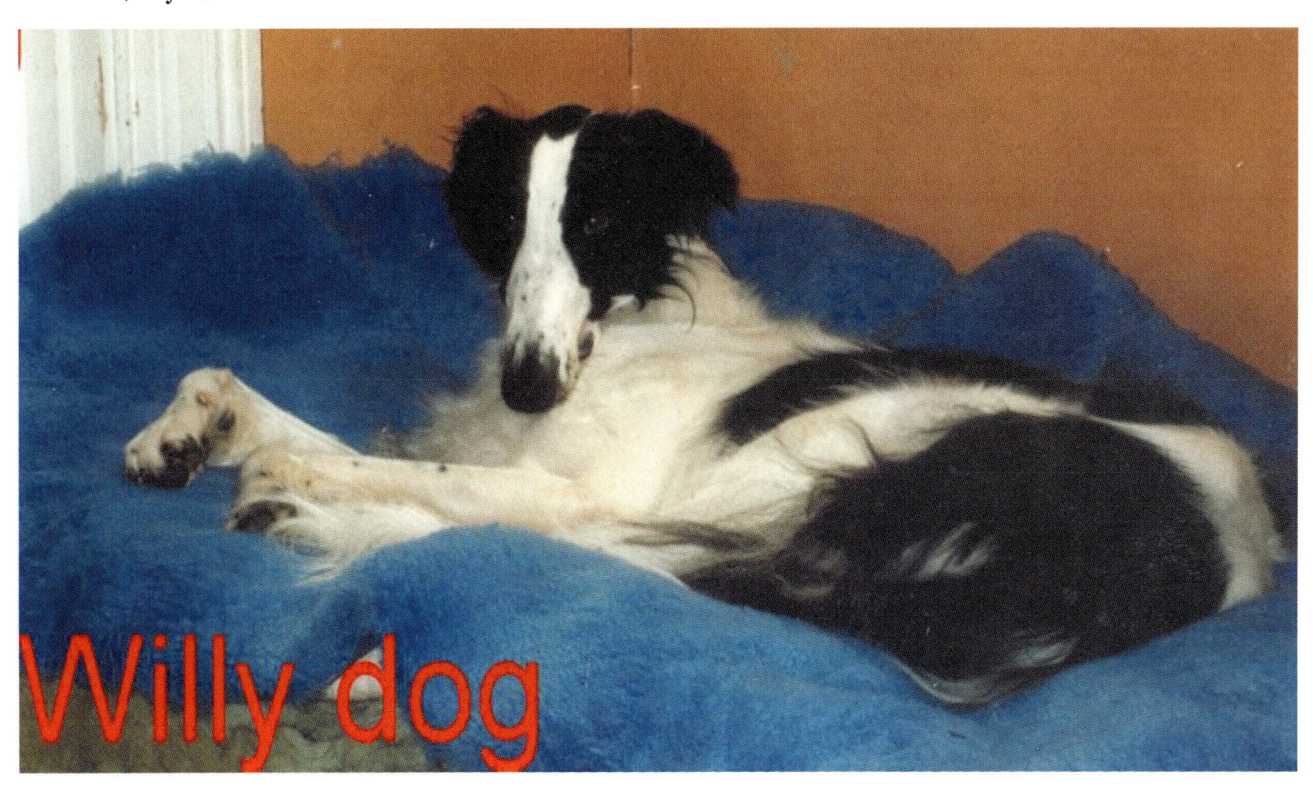

Willy dog

I was so bothered about Williams story that I decided to write it from his what might have been his point of view. At the time of doing this, I did not know the part the vet played in it, if I had done, I think the story would have been somewhat different.

I did however, get my revenge on her. A couple of years after I had taken William in, I stayed with Carol in Dubai, on the way home from visiting my son in Bali.

I asked Carol if I could meet this woman, Carol, sensing trouble, was not at all keen, but I assured her that I would be nothing but sweetness and charm. We met for coffee and chatted away about nothing in particular. When it was time for us to leave, I said to her, (do not forget, she never knew what had happened to William). "I owe you such a big thank you". She looked at me in surprise, "But we have never met before". "I know" I said "but what a wonderful job you did on that Borzoi's legs. He lives with me and has become the leading Borzoi in the show ring; winning more C.C.'s than any Borzoi has ever done before. He is also being used at stud and is earning me an absolute fortune". All lies I know, but the look on her face was well worth it. Revenge is sweet and I did it for you, my beloved boy.

This is what I wrote, how it might have been.

Somehow, I know that life has been like this before: happy, secure, loving. I have a very distant memory - not too clear, perhaps, is all so long ago - of warmth and comfort. Of my mother, snuggling close to her, drinking milk from her. The warmth of her body. Her silky coat to snuggle into, my brothers and sisters - how many I cannot now remember - pressing close, all of us together. I knew nothing else, nor did I want to; I expected life to always be like this.

As I grew a little older and my eyes opened, I became aware that I wasn't alone in my little world. There were strange creatures that stood up straight on to back legs made odd, harsh sounds, not pleasant like a gentle whimpering of my mother, or the cries we all gave when we were hungry or wanted to press closer to our mother. I soon became aware that my mother was afraid of these strange creatures and their odd noises; her body would grow stiff and an odd rumbling sound would emerge from her throat. I wished she wouldn't - when she did this the noise from the creatures became louder and they would waive their front legs about at my mother, making us pups scream with terror and press as close as we could to her.

I don't remember too much of what our home was like. I do remember that unless we stayed very close together, we were very cold, and what we lay on was hard and uncomfortable. This was particularly difficult for our mother, who began to get sore spots all over her, which wasn't helped by us youngsters crawling all over her, my mother told me this place was a shed. It was very dark; in fact, there wasn't in lot of difference after my eyes had opened! Our mother was always hungry; occasionally the door would open, which let in a shaft of light that hurt my eyes and made us blink. Then at one of these "people" mother said they were called that - would throw her a bone to gnaw on, or a piece of fish that was usually frozen; so, too, was the water, which was particularly hard for mother and she was always so thirsty. We youngsters were all right at the start as mother provided us with lovely, warm milk, but eventually that came in short supply, so we too became very hungry.

Then came the dreadful day when all this was to change. I shall never forget it, it was the first time I was to know real fear. Two of these people came into our shed, making a lot of noise and pulling us about, picking us up, poking and prodding none too gently, turning us upside down, holding us by the loose skin on our necks … … … that hurt, and some of my sisters cried out in fear. Our mother became distraught, barking and growling, pleading with the people not to hurt her babies; they didn't seem to understand, and instead struck out at her, making her real backwards, banging her head hard against the back of the shed. She lunged forward again, still trying to protect us, but this time they caught her, threw a sack over her head and pushed her out to the door, banging it shut behind her. That was the last time I ever saw my mother; her cries of anguish echoed in my ears.

Roughly they picked me up and threw me into a small box, banging the lid down hard. I lay there in the dark, too frightened to even try to move. I wanted my mother; I began to scream for her. Suddenly the box was opened; "mother?" But it was not her; instead, one of my brothers was thrown in beside me. We clung together terrified, and our lives changed forever. They threw our box into a car and drove off with us.

This misery seemed to last forever. We were slipping and sliding all over the place inside a little dark prison. By now we were thirsty, but no one gave us anything. We cried for our mother, her comforting milk. Eventually we heard one of the people say, "10 kilometers to Kiev". Was this to be our new home? Was our mother there? How wrong we were … … …

The car stopped, our box was picked up, and we felt ourselves been carried - slipping and sliding and shaking with fear. There was so much noise, so many people shouting. A box was taken away, thrown on another moving machine on which we rode for a bit, and then that, too, stopped, and we were again lifted up. The next thing we knew, we seemed to be lifted into the air, and then we landed with a thud. Silence. My brother and I huddled as close together as possible, terrorized. Then the box was opened for a brief instant and a bowl of water was at last slipped in. We drank desperately and soon finished it.

As we cried together, wondering was next to come, the most terrifying roaring noise began! If we were frightened before, we were mortified now. The roar grew steadily louder, and all around us things began to shake and shudder; then we felt ourselves moving, going faster and faster; then arrived the most extraordinary sensation, we felt as though we were going up in the air. Our box began to slide about, banging into who knows what; it was a living nightmare for us. Slowly though, we felt ourselves straightening out and things were less noisy.

Many hours must have passed, I do not know how many, when suddenly we felt like we were dropping downwards. There was a horrible and roaring noise again, followed by a big bang! As we hit the ground, and the horrible box began to shake and shudder and we stopped moving altogether. Silence. We hardly dare breathe.

Again time passed as my brother and I pressed together for comfort. Then a box was lifted and again came that horrible swinging movement; we felt ourselves being lowered again on to a moving object. I remember the heat at the time - it was unbearable. Then the box started moving and we were placed on the ground. The surrounding noise was awful, but the heat was horrendous, and we were so thirsty and so very hungry again. I felt odd, as if I were floating, it was wonderful; mother was with us, looking after us and feeding us as I passed into blackness. Peace … … … At last.

I was out of the box and a man was holding me. The room was large but OH! So hot! He gave me blessed water to drink and I felt my mother going away again, leaving me so alone and afraid. Then my eyes cleared; mother wasn't there. I looked around. I was in yet another box, but with this one I could look around out of the front, and it was much larger. I looked at my surroundings and how strange they were … … lots of open boxes like mine with odd-looking occupants in them. Mostly were like my kind, only they had much shorter legs and none possessed the beautiful long, silky coat of my mother.

I felt a little grander that moment, and then I saw the look of misery in their eyes; I then knew in this new Hell we were all equals. Then I panicked was my brother no longer with me. Eventually

I saw him in a cage like mine, right beside me. I was relieved, we were still together. I call to him but he didn't seem hear me, he just lay there with his eyes closed, not even panting in this terrible heat. I got angry at him; he could at least talk to me, comfort me.

Then my cage door opened and a "people" picked me up. There were actually two of them; they were much smaller than those of my home country of Russia. They hugged and stroked me, patted my head. It felt good and I relaxed. Then they started to carry me away. "My brother", I screamed. "We Are Together … … don't please don't leave him behind!" they didn't seem to understand. I know it wasn't my fault that I left him there - my last link to my puppy hood - but how can I stop the pain that I felt?

These more people carried be out to a car; they climbed into the back, laid me across their laps, and gently stroked my head, put their faces close to mine, hugging me so tight. It was wonderfully cool and I began to relax. Sometime later, the car stopped and I was lifted out and carried through a door down a long passage, into a large, airy room. I was put down gently and I stared with amazement at my surroundings. So much light and space, so cool, so many wonderful looking beds to lie on! I trotted towards one and tried to climb up, but it was too high for me. One of the little ones lifted me on to it and it was bliss; I sank into the softest bed I had ever been on.

They bought me milk to drink and little bits are sweet-tasting meat which I ate with speed. I was so very tired, and so drifted off into a troubled sleep. I kept seeing my brother, he was looking for me; I kept calling to him but he didn't hear me, he just went on crying for me. Suddenly he saw me and began shouting loudly as he ran towards me. Just as he was about to reach me, the noise became louder, and my brother seemed to fade from me as I struggle to reach him; the shouting was coming from more people who had entered the room. The little people were crying and holding on to me, and the new ones were big, like the others I had known. These two bent down and roughly grab me up, pulling me from the arms of the crying children. Relentlessly they carried me away, outside into the heat, and then threw me none too gently into the back of the car. "Get rid of him," commanded the man who was driving the car. "Anyway that you want."

The man roughly pulled me by the loose skin of my neck through to the seat beside him. It hurt badly and I cried out, which caused him to hit me hard on the side of my face. No comforting hands here! We drove off at speed and I crouch there, once again terrified. After an age, we slowed down somewhat and the man leaned across me and open the door beside me. Before I realized what was going to happen, he had pushed me HARD, I lost my balance and fell through the open door, crashing onto the hard roadside. The car sped away. An agonizing pain seared through both of my front legs and; I screamed out in agony and tried to stand up, but my front legs gave way, providing such pain that I was desperate. The heat was appalling, and I couldn't move. I do not know how long I lay there and in the end I did not even care as blackness overtook me.

Gentle hands stroked my head; I was lying on something soft. A quiet voice said, "he's coming round, poor little mite, both his front legs are smashed. He can't be more than six weeks old; this must be one of those poor Borzois that have arrived in to Dubai from Russia. It breaks my heart to see such cruelty; I'll have to operate on those legs." another voice said, "He isn't strong enough to survive the surgery. And even if he were, what future is there for him in this country?" "I'm here to save lives not to take them away", was the reply. Through their haze I felt a sharp prick on my neck and then I seem to drift into blessed oblivion.

My mind began to clear some time later, and again I found gentle hands stroking my head. A quiet, soft voice whispered to me. I tried to move, to stand up, but my front legs felt strangely heavy. I glanced down at them and saw something white and heavy wrapped around both of them. "Poor little boy," the gentle voice whispered. I was so tired I couldn't keep my eyes open any longer and again I drifted off into a deep sleep. The next few days were quiet and peaceful; my legs, with their heavy plaster on them, were uncomfortable but not unbearable. I was fussed over and given love and kindness; I had plenty of food and water, and began to feel stronger. I longed to run and stretch myself, but the plaster was too restricting.

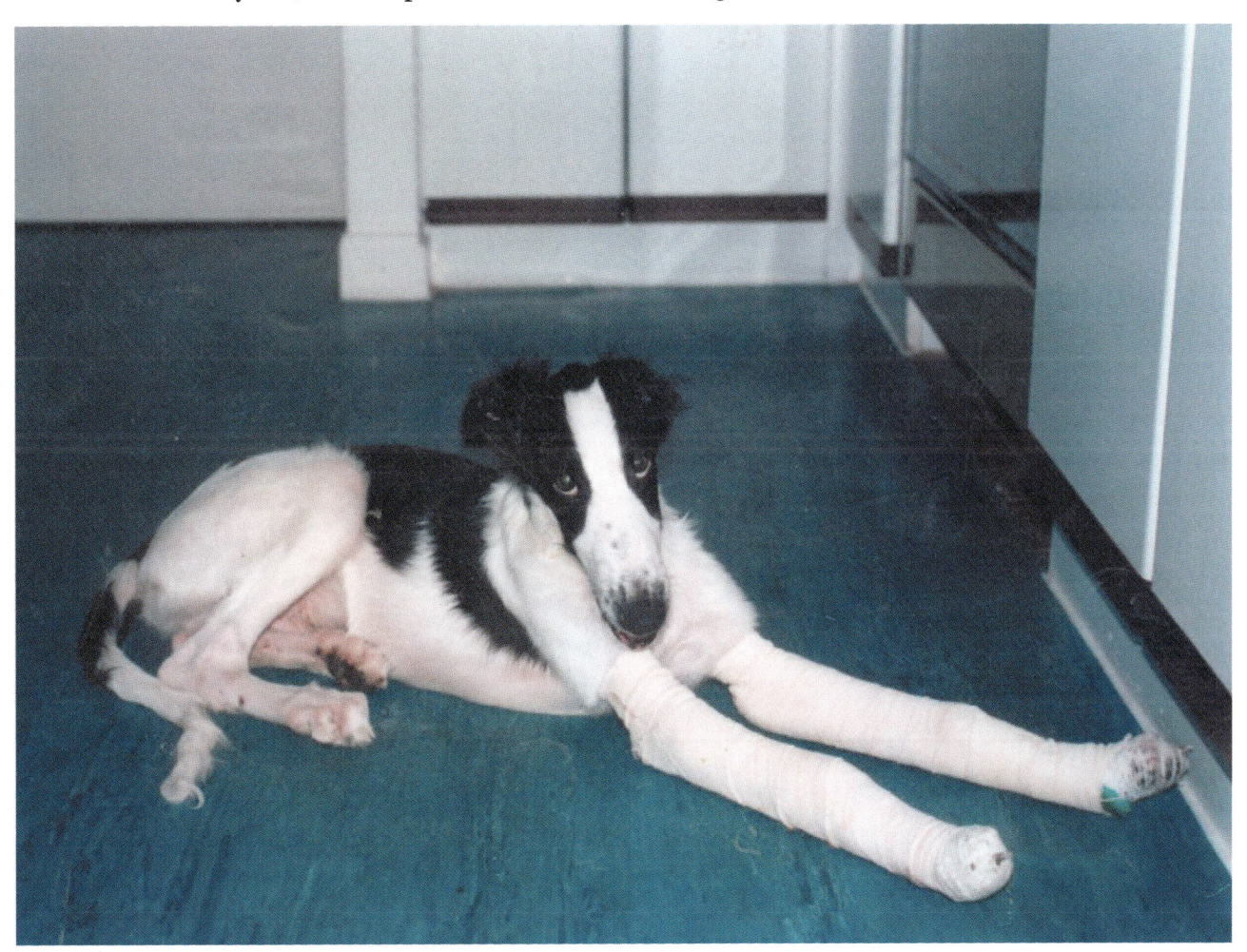

Then one day everything changed. I was lying on my bed dozing when a strange lady came in. She listened with sadness when she was told my story. "May I pick him up?" she asked. She lifted me gently on to her lap and began to caress me, speaking to me in a quiet, gentle voice. I loved her straight away and snuggle close to her by licking her face. She looked down at me, water glistening in eyes.
"How can this puppy be so trusting to people after all he has been through?" she enquired. "Why don't you take him home, Sheila?" said another lady. "He deserves a good home after all he has been through." the lady called Sheila nodded her head and pressed her face close to mine. There seem to be even more water coming from her eyes, and it made my face all wet.
I lay on her lap, keeping as close to the lady as I could. After a while, she stood up, holding me, and carried me to her car, placing me gently down on the seat beside her. I could not help feeling apprehensive and frightened, as I remembered the last time I was in one of these things. "Be lucky, little chap," said the other lady. "I will see you soon to take your plasters off."

With that, she drove me away and I started my new life, and what a life! It was better than I could ever imagine! When we got to her home, Sheila introduced me to Terry, and told me he would be helping to take care of me. I later learned these kind people were Sheila and Terry Williamson. I think perhaps that's why they named me William! I felt so loved, so safe with them. Sometimes I thought of my brother and wondered if he had been so lucky. I did hope so.

Sheila took me several times to the place I'd been before, and I learned it was called the vets. The people there were always very kind to me, but I was always pleased to get back into the car with Sheila and go home.

One day Sheila took me to the vets and she seemed very excited about it. Soon I discovered why, as my vet friend, with something very sharp in her hand, began to cut away the heavy stuff from my front legs. In no time at all, first one leg and then the other was free and lighter again. Everyone kept looking at my legs and admiring and saying "what a wonderful job".

After that, life was even better. My legs felt strong, and the freedom to run made life complete. The only thing that bothered me was the heat, as it was just too hot to move around in much, much as I wanted to. In fact, Sheila would keep me indoors in cool air for most of the time, but certainly she understood my need for exercise; every morning she would get out of bed before the sun came up, put me in the car, and drive me someplace she called "the beach". It was wonderful there! I could gallop there over the sand, no restrictions, just do what I wanted. Sheila didn't seem to mind if I was covered in sand or wet from the water; in fact she seemed to encourage me by throwing sticks for me to chase. My life was all that I wanted. I never thought it would change again …

… but I should have known. Every time I had been happy, something has gone wrong for me. Looking back, I cannot believe I didn't sense a problem; I was aware of tension, but I didn't think it concerned me.

Then one morning she held me tight, tighter than I felt comfortable; but, because I loved her, I sensed no fear, even though her face was wet again. Terry entered the room, and the look she gave him made me get frightened again. I pressed against her fear taking over. "I love you," she cried in my ear. "I Will Always Love You. But you cannot stay here without us, so you are going to England where, some place, you will be happy again. My promise to you, William. I know it is for the best." Terry pulled me from her gently while the water from my eyes fell down her face. I licked at it to make her better. She turned from me, saying, "go, Terry, please go." not realizing or understanding that yet again my life was going to change … … forever.

The full horror of what was happening to me became clear once we got to a destination. It was as before, the noise, the shoving, the pushing! Fear took hold.

Terry placed me gently in a large box (oh please, no, not again!), then put his arms around me. Water was on his face, too. I licked him, he pulled away and suddenly he was gone. Despair.. … total despair. All was the same as before, the horrendous whining in the air with the terrifying noises. I wanted my brother; where was my brother?!

My crate was certainly more comfortable than the one I was in before; there was more room in it, plenty of fresh water, and even some food. But I did not feel like eating, I felt so abandoned, so alone and frightened. Sheila, Terry, how could you do this to me … … I thought you loved me! I hunched up in misery at the back of the crate; the journey was endless.

At last I felt that dropping down movement. I tensed up even more than before and waited, trembling, not knowing what the future held for me.

Hours later, after being left alone in my box in a shady corner, I drifted into a troubled sleep despite my unease. I woke to hear a quiet voice, "Hello, old boy, come on, we'll take care of you." my box was lifted on to a trolley and wheeled to a waiting van. Once put inside, I was given fresh water and a little food; but I still wasn't hungry. The van started up and we were off, where to I had no idea. Sheer exhaustion washed over me again, and I fell asleep dreaming of Sheila and Terry.

The sight of my new surroundings on our arrival did little to lift my spirits; all I could see was rows of long, narrow runs with dogs are various shapes and sizes living inside, barking and making as much noise as they could. What's more, none looked even remotely like me. I pulled back feeling frightened and unsure of myself, but my handler was insistent; he placed me firmly inside one of these long pens, shutting the door on me. A bit confused at first, I turned my head and saw another part to the pound, one with an open door. I went through this door and discovered a bed covered with a rug; this was where I was to sleep.. … A far cry from Sheila and Terry's. This place was to be my home for six entire months. I later discovered it was called "quarantine". I had arrived in England.

Once settled in and used to this life, I'll admit it wasn't so bad. The worst part was the restriction and not being able to stretch my growing limbs, to gallop and to run free. There were several people they're looking after us dogs and they were all very kind and gentle. But I still long for Sheila and Terry and every time I heard a car arrived I would run to the side of my pen to see if they come to get me; of course, they never did. As weeks and months dragged by, I began to think of them less; the memories faded and, strangely enough, this enabled me to settle better.

After I'd been there a few weeks, two strange ladies came to see me. They made a great fuss of me, patting me, admiringly. It felt good. "He must be about eight months," one said to the other. They weren't far off, either! I hoped they had come to take me in their car, but instead they left without me. Alone, again.

Life returned to normal, but a few weeks later one of these ladies returned; she bought me a really big bone, the biggest I've ever seen. I'll tell you, I couldn't wait to get my teeth around that one.

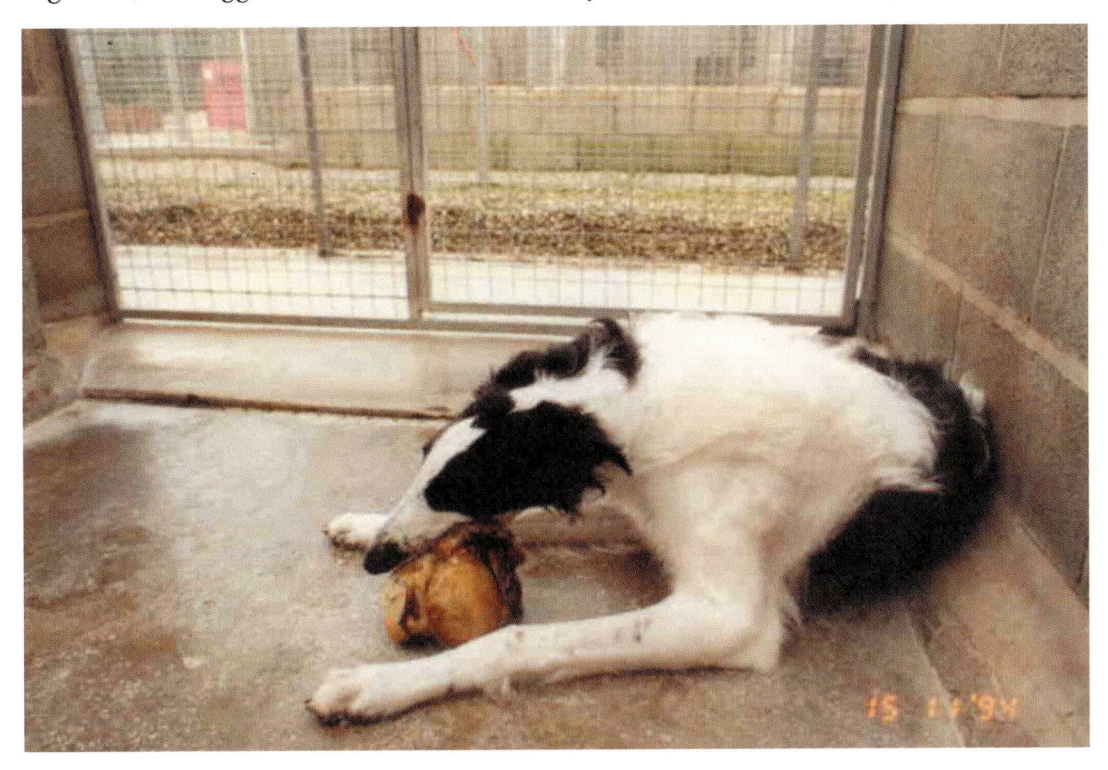

She also bought me a big, fluffy rug which she put on my bed. I couldn't wait to sink my teeth into that either, but I managed to wait until she was gone. She stayed with me for quite a while that day, talking to me and petting me, and again I wondered if she would take me home with her. Again she left without me, however, so I took my frustration out on her rug, ripping it into pieces! She repeated these visits two or three times more, and I always felt let down when she drove away leaving me behind.

One day, things appeared different. One of the girls who look after all of us took me out of my pen to a room I had never seen. She closed the door behind us, and the next thing I knew, water was being poured all over me! I was apparently having my first bath, and I sincerely hope it will be my last. Being dried and brushed was quite nice, though, and I admit it felt really good to be clean, though a good roll in something nice and smelly wouldn't go amiss … … I seem to get extra attention from everyone that day; people were passing me and hugging me, saying "Goodbye" to me. I was apprehensive. Though this wasn't an ideal home, at least I felt safe here and knew no one would ever hurt me. The rest of that day passed without incident, and that night as I a curled up on my bed I relaxed once again.

Next day, my lady visitor arrived again, and this time I couldn't believe what was happening! One of the helpers put the lead on me and let me out of my run across the garden to where the visitor was standing. To my amazement, she opened her car door, and I jumped right in! "You're going home, William." she said. Could I believe this? Could I trust her? We drove a long-distance, but there was plenty of room in the car and it was lovely to travel loose and not in a box. After several hours, the car slowed down and the road was twisty. Then we stopped altogether and the lady said, "Your home, William home at last!"

I was eager to jump out of the car to see what home was, but she held on to me firmly, saying, "you have to meet the others, first." what others, I wondered. I was soon to find out!

I was led into a large garden with a wall all way round it. She closed a gate firmly behind us, and it was then that I saw them. They came rushing towards me, three beautiful dogs I couldn't believe it, they looked just like me! They rushed over and I was suddenly afraid. What if they didn't like me! I froze, not sure what to do. One of these dogs, a boy, was really big, much bigger than I was. I drew back, pressing against the lady. He sniffed me and wagged his tail. I wagged back, and then the other two, both girls, came over to me, and had a good sniff, and then dismiss me, playing with the boy.

My new lady let go of my lead and hesitantly I trotted off to inspect my new home. There was more to come, too. After a short while, I was put back on the lead and led into the house. Two more Borzoi shot off chairs and rushed at me for several minutes, make me feel very nervous again; but after a time and one final, dirty look at me, they march back off to their chairs.

Six months have passed since that particular day. I am so settled now with my family; I play endlessly with all the others, even Vodka, well mum told me to be careful with her as she is "top dog". My best friend is the big boy, Blue, or Sholwood Singing the Blues to give him his smart name.

On second thoughts, my really best friend is my mum, who tells me how much she loves me that I will never leave here; that I would never suffer, or be lonely and frightened again.
And do you know what? I think I really believe her! Yes, this is my "tail told to wag"!!!

I do admit to being nervous about taking William in. Living on my own, I felt six Borzoi, all in the house, was probably rather too many, but, I thought, in for a penny, in for a pound!
Also, I was extremely lucky, as I had Milan, who had handled Blue at Crufts, staying with me, for a few days, so he was here to dog sit the others while I was away and help me with the introductions when I got home. I needn't have worried, you would think they had all known each other all their lives!
William was a delight in every way, his character was just unfaultable. He was such a happy dog and he just loved people.
I sometimes took him to the Borzoi club shows, "Not for competition", he loved it, but I did have to anchor him down. If he could, he would go walk about, visiting as many people as he could, sticking his nose in their faces, or their sandwiches. His favourite trick though, was to get into the ring, which, in the middle of judging, could be rather embarrassing!
To this end though, I used to appease him. When the judging broke for lunch, with the help from a few friends, I would take William into the ring with a few others and their dogs, while someone would judge us. William of course always won! I swear he knew it; he had an expression on his face, resembling a big grin. It was magic! What a character!
As he grew older, his poor front legs grew very bandy

and he developed a very wobbly gait, but for all that it did not seem to make any difference to his enjoyment of life.

William left me in 2004, he went downhill quickly, which I suppose I have to be thankful for, but what a gap he has left. He was so different from the others, in so many ways. If we had been on holiday, or even out for a few hours, he was the only one who would bother to come through and greet us. He adored the car, I didn't take him very often, as it would normally be runs into my local supermarket, and even in the winter, if the sun is out, it can get too warm if he was left for any length of time, also we have a lot of dog thieves in this area, a locked car does not seem to bother them, but, Oh! How I had to sneak out. The car keys hang on a board in the kitchen, however quiet I was picking them up, he heard and would come rushing through. I couldn't bare the look on his face, when I left without him. He always forgave me though, with the greeting I got on my return.

The other laugh about him, was his musical talent, he loved to "sing", very loudly, to various theme tunes that came on the television, by "singing" with him, you could keep him going several minutes after the music had finished! It was quite a noise!

When he left me, as my vet put the needle in his arm, the last thing I heard from him, was the faintest sound of that beloved song.

My wonderful, wonderful Wills, all my dogs were unforgettable, but there will never be one like you again. I just pray there is a "Rainbow Bridge", he will be there before all the others to meet me.

All I can say now is thank you Terry and Sheila Williamson, for trusting me with this wonderful dog, for taking him in, in the first place and for smuggling him out of Dubai.

Here they are together, Terry and William, the last time they met, the last goodbye, a wonderful dog and a caring man.
Please God, let your tail still be wagging, my beloved William.
William possessed,
"Courage without ferocity, strength without insolence, and all the virtues of man, without his vices
"Lord Byron" In memory of Boatswain, a Newfoundland dog

Chapter 13, Gentle's Story

Since my husband's death, I had been under pressure from my accountant, to make a decision on a property that he had had plans to restore. Whether to go ahead with his plans, or put the house on the market as it was. I was somewhat undecided about this, but after several months, I decided to sell it, as it was. I rang my accountant, who lives a long way from here, to tell him of my decision. Probably less than an hour later, my telephone rings. A male voice apologised for ringing and introduced himself to me. He then explained he was interested in looking at the house, as he had heard it was for sale. Well!! I knew news travels fast, but this was unbelievable!
He asked if he could call round and collect the key. I was thoroughly irritated by this and very nearly said no, but remembering I was going to sell, agreed. When "Martin" arrived, I gave him the key and, very icily said he was to return it by six o'clock, as I had other people looking at it later on! He returned it punctually and, having calmed down somewhat, asked him in for a drink, which he accepted. On entering the sitting room, he really put his foot in it. In each chair and sofa, was draped a beautiful Borzoi. Now, I am used to people saying, what beautiful dogs, or words to that affect. Martin looked at them and said, "Personally, I am a cat man myself"! Martin never did buy my house, but three years later, he married me!! He is now a dog man! Gentle was a wedding present! We called her Gentle, because, while our love blossomed, we had two special songs, one of which was Dean Martin's "Gentle on my Mind".

We planned Gentle's arrival very carefully. Martin loves his shooting and wanted a gundog, for my wedding present to him, I bought him a Flatcoat Retriever, who was the same age as Gentle. We went to Hampshire to pick him up, arriving home ten minutes before Gentle's breeder arrived with her.

We kennelled them together and they became firm friends. Sadly though, none of my other Borzoi liked her. Skye and Vodka were particularly nasty and I never let them be alone together. In hindsight, I should have returned Gentle to her breeder, but we struggled on and, now that Skye and Vodka have left me, she is a happy contented little girl.

From the day she arrived, she was always nervous; her breeder had to carry her, to get her out of the car. Maybe, this was why the others had no time for her. I did try and show her, but she was so upset by it all, I realised it was cruel to continue.

Life has not been fare to her, she is eight years old, as I write this and last year, she began to develop a film over both eyes. My vet referred her to the Animal Health Trust, a wonderful place a few miles from me. She saw the eye specialist there who diagnosed (must get the correct name for this, on her return there in July)?? Thanks to this lovely lady, her eyes will get no worse, left untreated, she would have gone blind. Her vision is impaired, but is reasonable and for the rest of her life, she will have to have eye drops, which she is very good about. To start with, she had to go to the Animal Health Trust once a week, now it is only every six months.

She is very set in her ways, preferring to spend the major part of her time in her kennel, desperately sadly, without Lima, the Flatcoat. One dreadful night, he squeezed under the gate and I found him, dead by the main road.

She does though, prefer to sleep in the house at nights and, I welcome this with open arms. One thing she does hate though, is Chasqui, Lima's replacement, if she could kill him, she would! I suppose she feels it is poetic licence after all she went through with Skye and Vodka.

I am glad I kept her, simply, we love each other.

Around this time, I realised I was going to have to sell my beloved Stradishall, it was costing just too much to carry on. I was lucky in the fact that I had Martin's house to move into. My main worry was moving my dogs and, Gentle was one that I worried about. With her nervous disposition and her failing eye sight, I realised it was going to be so hard for her.

One afternoon, I was taking the dogs out, Gentle didn't really want to come, but I persuaded her. We went only a short walk and slowly, just as we got nearly back, her hind legs gave way and she collapsed. I went to get a towel to support her with, but when I got back to her, she had got up and was making her wobbly way home. I got her safely on her bed and she seemed to recover. I never walked her again, just let her out when she felt like it. Then a few weeks before the move was due, I came down one morning to find her spread eagled on the kitchen floor. Her legs had gone again. I managed to get her back on her bed, and prayed she would recover like last time. She did not, and I knew what I had to do.

I miss her so much, but, I feel thankful she was spared the move.

Chapter 14, Frost and Fialka's Story

It was in May 2002, when things went wrong for another Borzoi breeder.
She was taken to court by the R.S.P.C.A. The outcome being that she had to find homes for several of her dogs.
I was sitting in the kitchen, with a Borzoi friend, who was over from America, we were tucking into the wine, when the 'phone rang, it was this breeder, extremely distressed, asking me to give a home to one of her dogs. I could see my friend had caught the gist of my conversation, she was shaking her head and mouthing "no", but the wine was talking, I said "yes"! My friend pointed out how foolish I was, that I had the perfect pack set up here, as far as my Borzoi were concerned and bringing in another one, might destroy the whole thing.
This gave me food for thought, two are easier than one! Another glass later, I rang the breeder back and told her I would home two.
I broke the news to Martin, who was very reasonable about it, that made a really pleasant change, from the type of reaction I would have had in the past! The next morning though, when I woke, I had definite cold feet. I told Martin that I had changed my mind. His reaction amazed me; he rounded on me, saying, "When I married you, I thought you were a woman of your word." "I am", I said "but I just can't cope with two more." "I'm here and I will help you". That was the end of the discussion.
A friend with large kennels had been boarding many of these dogs, including mine, until permanent homes could be found, agreed to bring them to me. I have a theory that if new dogs arrive with someone, as so many people have stayed here with their dogs, that they think they are only temporary and the introductions pass over peacefully. Sadly, that theory didn't work with Gentle, but it did in this case.

She stayed overnight, helping to settle them in their kennel and walked them with the others on our morning walk. All went well, but I could see they were nervous of both Martin and me.
After she left to go home, I realised they were not just nervous but terrified.
They huddled together, behind the back door, where Blue and Skye slept at night, literally shaking with fear.

I felt so sorry for them and realised too, I had big problems ahead. Letting them out of their kennel in the morning, was a nightmare. If I didn't put their leads on before I opened the door of the run, I knew I would not be able to get near them. I had been told, they would never take anything from our hands, all my dogs go to bed with a chocolate finger each, theirs I had to put on their bed, but, slowly, slowly, they came round. Now, they grab the finger from my hand and, Martin's, who always gives them a chew, before the morning walk.
Frost was the easiest one to get to know and soon showed me that she liked a cuddle or two. Fialka though, took her time, but Oh! It was worth the wait. The expression on her face and look in her eyes is pure joy, when I let them out in the mornings. No leads now! She goes charging off at the rate of knots, her tail flowing, straight into the house, to see what has been left in the kitchen, from the night before. Frost though, before she rushes indoors, always puts her front feet on my shoulders and gives me a good morning kiss!
During the day, when they get home from their walk, they go straight to the sitting room, where they remain until it is time for their afternoon walk. Not even the vacuum cleaner, going right up to their bean bags, disturbs them. Fialka may occasionally open one eye, but that is as far as it goes!
I have even managed to get Frost in the Show ring, with one credible first and various placings She even managed to impress a Russian judge, who was judging Borzoi's , he placed her and told me, if it hadn't been for my handling, she would have won the class!!. The next show I went to, he was there, I let him handle her, and they came fifth out of five!

I just don't know what I would do without these two and Gentle. Having had so many all together, I now have so few. I cannot thank Martin enough, for not letting me change my mind.

As I write this, I have had some devastating news about Fialka. She had developed a very dirty ear, it did not seem to bother her, but I didn't like the look of it, so I called in my vet, who cleaned it and found a small mole like, lump in her ear. She strongly advised me to have it removed. I did not like this idea, being so nervous, I thought taking her to the surgery, would be devastating for her. I gave in eventually, as my vet agreed to come here and sedate her before we took her there. All went well, the lump was removed and she was home with me in no time.

A few days later came the shock, it was malignant. The option was to have the entire ear removed. I was shocked. I have thought and thought about this and have come to the decision, this is not an option. Fialka is eight years old, so happy now and settled, I just can't put her through this drastic surgery. I have asked many Borzoi friends for their advice and not one has disagreed with me. I look at her now, running across the lawn, jumping the Haa Haa, laughter in her eyes, I just pray she stays this way for some time yet. When things start to go wrong, I know what to do.

Several months later disaster struck her again, a final cruel blow.

Fialka developed pyometra and had to be operated on. I had noticed recently that she had been slightly lame, and asked my vet to investigate this, while she was under the anaesthetic. I had not been too concerned, as I had seen the Flatcoat run into her and knock her over, a few days before and thought this the cause. I was utterly gutted when Sally rang me and told me it was bone cancer. She asked, should she put her down then and there. My reply was one word, no. A decision I do not regret.

She coped so bravely with this terrible disease, in the end, she could not put that leg to the ground, but still enjoyed her walks, managing so well on three legs, still enjoyed her food, but my guide line was the sparkle in her eyes, while she had that, I knew life was still good for her.

Then one morning, I was cuddling her, when I felt a further lump on her ribs, my heart sank as I suspected the cancer had travelled to her lungs.

I suspect I was right, she began to blow on her walks, and I found it kinder too, to walk on grass, keeping her off the road as much as possible.

On that last evening, she did not want to go to her kennel at bed time, so I left her in the house. When I came down stairs the following morning, she had moved on to a bed by the back door. She wanted to go out, but cried out in pain. I could see the sparkle had gone. She went straight to her kennel, where she lay, frightened and in pain. She went to sleep in my arms.

A short time after she died, I received a note from a lady who had been treating her with radionics, I feel her words are a fitting epitaph.

"I am so proud of Fialka. I feel she did so well and lived her life so well and so full. I hope you are proud of her too. What a strong spirit, and what a privilege we have meeting her. I love the Tagore saying: Death is not extinguishing the light; it is putting out the lamp because dawn has come. This is so true of Fialka."

A last little smile, before I come to the end of my "Dog Tails".

I have always loved black Borzoi; it is definitely my favourite colour.

One day, sitting in the hairdressers, I was talking about my dogs and describing them to my hairdresser. The lady next door to me came out from under the hair drier, in time to hear me say. "I am mad about blacks, I find them completely irresistible". The look on her face, was worth a guinea a minute!!

Chapter 15, Borzoi revisited.

Choo Choo and Sapphira, their stories.

Well, I might have known it! Three Borzoi would never be enough for me!
Slowly slowly, the idea formed in my somewhat one tracked mind.
I wanted somehow, to have a connection with Skye, Blue and Mouse. One name kept creeping into my mind, British and American Champion, Stillwater Virginia Reel, their grandmother. The more I thought, the more I liked the idea. Life had become much kinder to imported dogs since Virginia's days. From many countries, including the USA, quarantine had been replaced by the "Pet Passport Scheme". The dog has to stay at the kennel, or home that it is at, for the allotted six months, be micro chipped, rabies vaccinated and de fleaded, in that order and the paperwork is horrendous, no mistake can be made, as, on arrival here, if all is not correct, the dog will not be allowed to enter the country.
Eventually, I made up my mind and in June 2005, I e-mailed Chuck Tyson, to see how he felt about this, and if he had anything he would sell me. I decided, as usual, two bitches would be easier than one.
Chuck and I had met briefly a few years before, and we had kept up a short e-mail correspondents, but really, he knew very little about me. I told him all I could think of, and sent him photographs of where they would live. His reply really touched me, "I really don't know why" he said, "but I

really feel I know you and you are different from the average Borzoi owner, I will be glad to let you have two of my girls". Wow! What a compliment.

Next, the decision ... What a task. I asked if there was a self black bitch, the answer was no, then a week or so later, yes! In her picture, she looked just like Mouse, BUT, her father was Sholwood Silver Fox, Blue's dad, I had to have her. I knew she was not young and that I would not be able to show her, but my basic need for a Borzoi is love, not the show ring.

First there was Peachessuch a pretty girl, I decided she was the one, until Chuck was kind enough to tell me her indentation could be a problem if I was going to show her, so, he sent me a picture of Choo Choo, and I fell in love!!

I think the deportation of these two girls must have been a big problem for Chuck and Virginia, they are both in their eighty's, and all that paperwork, so daunting.

One of the worst problems was the crates that they were to fly in. The rules dictated that the dog, standing in it's crate, with ears pricked, had to have an inch to spare above it. Borzoi have neat ears close to their heads. Chuck put Sapphira in the biggest crate he could find, and pulled her ears up for the authorities, had she pricked them, she couldn't pass the test ... Poor Chuck, he had to insert pieces of wood in the side of the crate to heighten it.

Above all, they agreed to fly with them, to help me settle them in. For this, I am just so grateful to them.

In the November of that year, Martin and I flew to Tennessee to meet the girls. We planned to visit on the day after we arrived, spend the day and one night with them. I was so excited, I just couldn't wait to meet them!

Choo Choo was fine, a friendly outgoing girl, Sapphira though, was a different story. She was terrified of both Martin and I. I could not get near her and when Chuck held her, so I could stroke her, she appeared ready to collapse with fear. I quickly realised that this was going to be a big, big problem, and I seriously doubted that it would be kind to move her, especially as she was seven years old. The trouble was, they were both well into their quarantine period, and if I chose another in her place, I would have to start all over again. I voiced my fears to Chuck, who convinced me she would soon settle, so I left things as they were.

On the 21st April 2006, Chuck, Virginia, Sapphira and Choo Choo arrived at Gatwick around 10.30 am. I was a complete nervous wreck, I had convinced myself that they had had torsion on the 'plane, and one or both were dead, or the paperwork would not be in order and they would be returned to the US, or put into quarantine for six months. What a doubting Thomas am I, as I write, two very happy girls are sleeping contentedly here, perfectly settled, loving their life … … … … Just SO glad I did it .

Chapter 16, Choo Choo's Story.

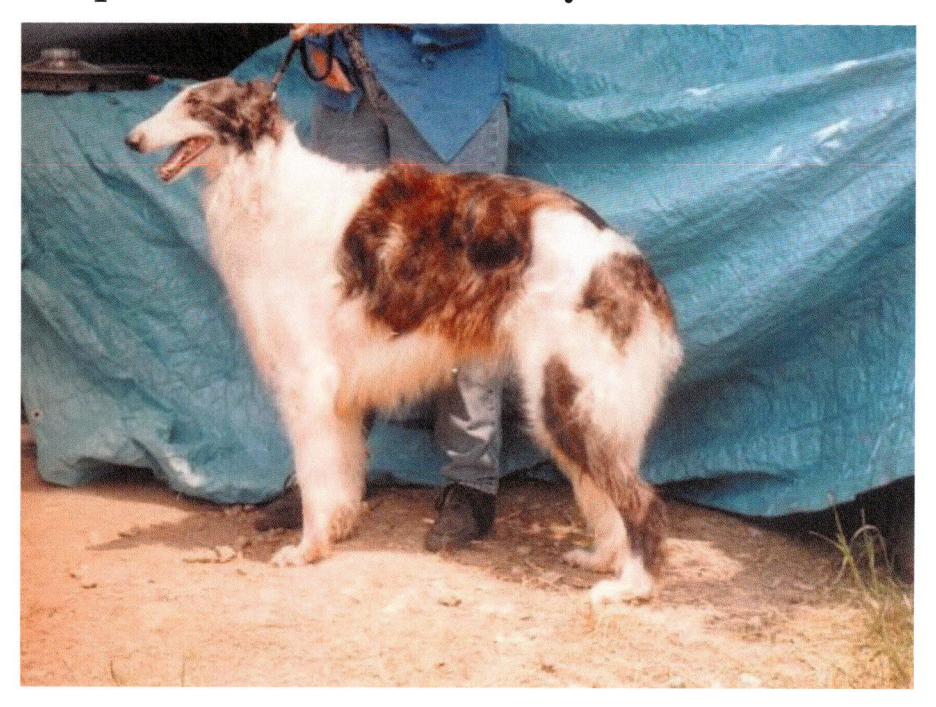

One of the first things I loved about Choo Choo was the marking of her near hind leg. It is the sort of marking you either love or hate.

The other thing about Choo Choo, she isn't really, when Chuck registered her with the American Kennel Club, by mistake he wrote Cho Cho! Once registered, you cannot change it, so, like it or not, we are stuck with it. This though, being my own private writings and not controlled by the Kennel Club, I am free to call her Choo Choo.

When she arrived on that traumatic day in April, she was three days into her fifth year, a great granddaughter of Virginia Reel, one generation further away from her than my beloved Duckworth Delinquents.

She does not remind me particularly of any of them, either in looks or character. Strangely enough, she has caught me out a few times, maybe it is a trick of light, or the way she moves, but more than once, she has walked into the room where I am, I look up and for a fleeting wonderful moment, I think, there's William. So for this reason, she is what I am looking for.

Her temperament is wonderful, she is soft and gentle, loves to be with me, infact Martin has christened her Limpet!

She has adapted well to the show scene, she hasn't had that magic first yet, but has never been lower than third. Her day will come! Except it never did. Somehow or other she managed to break one of her front toes and is inclined not to be sound, also, on the one occasion that I took her to a show with Filip, he just would not show, all he wanted was to be with her, so I thought it best to retire her.

She is such a sweet gentle dog, devoted to Sapphira and to me, in the mornings when I go out to greet them before their walk She literally dances towards me.

Chattanooga Choo Choo may you dance forever.

Chapter 17, Sapphira's story.

This picture of Sapphira, I took during my visit to Tennessee, I think it shows the fear in her eyes and maybe give some idea of how worried I was about bringing her home.

My first few weeks with her were agony for me and must have been dreadful for her. She was terrified of me and everyone else. I could not get near her, unless she was shut in the kennel. Shades of Frost and Fialka. I kept telling myself, if I can get through to them, then I can do it with Sapphira.

In the mean time though, I developed another problem. I learnt while in Tennessee that she had not been bred by Chuck, but bought from a German breeder, Edith Titse when she was six months old. This did not matter to me, as I have said, she was a daughter of Silver Fox, and a self black bitch, and my wanting her was purely sentiment. But what did matter to me and what I did not realise at the time, Edith had wanted to buy her back, and was obviously upset when, having been told she was not for sale, to learn that she had ended up with me.

Edith and I started a slightly frosty e-mail correspondents, I think Edith had every right to be upset, I certainly would have been. Slowly though, through e-mails, we became friends. Edith expressed a desire to come and see her, this I thoroughly encouraged. She was helpfulness itself and I learnt the cause of her fright. When Edith had shipped her to Tennessee, at six months old, at some point, her crate had fallen from a height with her inside. My God! If I had known that, I would NEVER have flown her here. In hindsight, I can say Thank God I did not know it. Poor little girl!

While Edith and I were making plans for her to come here, tragedy struck.

I had taken Choo Choo to a show, leaving Sapphira alone for the first time. When I got home, I could see Sapphira was far from right, I called my vet, who confirmed my worst fears of all times, she was blowing. The dreaded bloat, I suppose in all the years I have had Borzoi, I am so lucky this was my first experience of this killer problem.

My vet bundled her immediately into the back of her car, having telephoned her husband to get ready for surgery.

Several hours later, Sally 'phoned, she was not round from the operation yet, all had gone as well as it could, but … It was the worst case of torsion she had ever seen, and she truly did not expect her to survive.

My darling Sapphira, I put you through all this and now I have killed you, was all I could think. I e-mailed Edith, who sent me the most lovely e-mail card that she had put together from all Sapphira's family, her litter brothers and sisters, Silver Fox, etc. wishing her luck, when she sent this, I knew she had forgiven me.

The next morning, she was still with us, I really don't think Sally could believe it. She was far from out of the woods though and Sally became very concerned for her. Everything was normal, or as well as could be expected in the circumstances, but she was not picking up as she should be.

In the mean time, I noticed how depressed Choo Choo appeared, and a thought occurred to me. I telephoned Sally with my idea, Sally was surprised and unsure, saying she had never done this before, but was willing to give it a try. Within half an hour, Choo Choo was lying in the kennel alongside Sapphire. Just a short time later, Sapphira started out on the road to recovery!

It was only a few days before I was allowed to bring them home. Sally explained the operation to me. The stomach was very black and a very large part had had to be removed. The little that was left had been stapled to her side, this would make it impossible to blow again, what a relief, as I knew from other peoples experiences, once the dog had had torsion, there was a strong possibility that it would happen again and a second attack would almost certainly be fatal.

On a lighter note, while Sapphira was still under the anaesthetic, Sally said to Richard her husband, this dogs teeth are filthy and I am going to clean them. Richard expressed some surprise at this, considering she was most unlikely to live. "Well, at least she will die with clean teeth" she retorted!

Well, wonders of wonders, thanks to the skills of my vets, she lived with clean teeth!

Caring for her and nursing her through her convalescence, was time consuming, but worth every effort, she began to trust me, she had to, and we began to bond. To start with, she had four small meals, including soaked biscuit, a day. There was so little left of her stomach, that she could only take a little at a time, being a greedy girl though, she looked forward to this and was always eagerly waiting for me to feed her. I swear she came near to stamping her feet if I was late for one of her meals! Poor girl, she had endless medication, but was so good about taking it. Her recovery was amazingly rapid and today, she is a happy healthy dog, she has put on weight, her coat shines and best of the lot, when she sees me, her tail wags, the sight of that, never fails to send a rush of joy through me. I have put my mind at rest; I did do the right thing by her.

Sadly, she has developed lumps in all her mammary glands. The vet said the only thing was a complete mammary strip, which would mean two very big operations. I have said no to this, I know it would be too much for her, anyhow, we do not know if they are malignant.

My black beauty, may you be happy for the rest of your life.

I just pray she was, I think so. A few days before the end, on the way home from our walk, she slipped going up an incline on the lawn just before the entrance to home. I couldn't get her up, so panicking, I left her for a couple of minutes while I let the others in, when I turned to go back to her she was there coming towards me, oh! The relief! But not for long, two days later, I found her down in the yard. I tried, oh how I tried, she couldn't move. I sat with her, coaxing and trying to move her. An hour or so later, it started to rain, I covered her with water proof coats and wept. My vet arrived a bit later and my heart broke.

Chapter 18. My Changing Life

Not long after my Stillwater girls arrived, I began to realise it was not going to be possible to stay in my beautiful home. The upkeep of the house and property was devastating. There was no money to be made from breeding race horses on the small scale that I was breeding on and, despite taking in boarders, my accountant made it quite clear I could not keep going. This decision broke my heart, so many memories, it was heart breaking to say goodbye. The situation was not helped by the purchaser, who flatly refused to give me any assurance that she would not demolish my dog's graves. I had to leave behind eleven special souls, ten Borzoi and a Flatcoat.

I shall never forgive her for this. Even if she had lied to me, I never would have known and I would have been more at peace.

My last walk past them and my very final goodbyes, will never be forgotten.

My worries too about what this move would do to my dogs, kept me awake night after night. My darling Gentle was spared this trauma. Her health was deteriorating. She now lived permanently in the house and eventually stopped wanting to go for a walk. One afternoon I wrongly made her go for a short, slow walk. Nearly home, when her hind legs collapsed, I could not get her up, so ran to the house for help. By the time I got back to her, she had managed it on her own. I supported her with a towel under her tummy, and slowly we got back to the house. I never made her walk again, but she did manage to wobble in and out of the house when she felt like it.

The consequence of this meant I could no longer take her for her eye check ups and her eyes began to deteriorate.

One morning, not long before the dreaded move, I came down to find her unable to get up, having spread eagled on the kitchen floor.

I prayed and prayed, she would find the strength to get up, as she had done the first time. I had managed to get her on to her bed in the sitting room, but those prayers were never answered. I knew what I had to do.

In many ways, it was a great relief, I really do not think she would have coped with the move. Dearest girl, "For ever Gentle on my Mind".

So, myself and the three remaining Russkaya's packed their bags, climbed into the car, and I at least, wept tears of heartbreak, as I drove down my drive for the very last time. But they say, every cloud has a silver lining, and I found mine, as usual, in my beloved dogs, they never looked back!

We moved to Martin's very old and beautiful family home. He had restored the stable block, to make kennels for my girls, well, not Frosty, just my Stillwater babies. They took to their new home as though it was meant to be. Sapphira, over the coming weeks, changed out of all recognition, a really happy, smiley, laughing person, like beloved Fialka, I could see joy in her eyes.

Choo was as happy and laid back as she had ever been and Frost settled on her bed in the kitchen, as though she had been there all her life. I felt as though a black cloud had been lifted from my shoulders.

A few months before we moved, the beginning of another change came my way. Looking at other people's Borzoi web sites, I fell in love! My first thoughts were, Oh my God, he is just like my beloved Blue.

So taken was I by this dog, that I sent his breeder an e-mail telling her how impressed I was with him. Helena thanked me and we started corresponding. Eventually, she asked if I would like a copy of his pedigree, which she sent. I was staggered, his father was Stillwater Spirit of T' Tsars, a grandson of Virginia Reel. I felt I had come full circle.

Chapter 19. Filip's Story.

I really feel he was meant to be. After my disaster with my planned mating of Blue and Mouse, I shelved any plans for a litter, my heart was just not in it. Then, when I saw Berk and fell in love, my thoughts turned to Choo. If I could use Berk, I could tie up my lines, as well as bringing in some foreign blood from his mother's side. Helena and I discussed it and the possibility of her bringing him over. When that looked as though it was going to be difficult, we discussed the possibility of A I. That proved impossible. The Kennel Club would only give permission for this, if the bitch concerned, had a registered litter. Choo had had a litter, but all had died and had not been registered. My dream appeared to fade. But, as it had happened in the past with Mouse, my daughter put her spoke in! At the time, my computer was down and, worried about keeping in touch with Helena, I asked Maria to e-mail her and keep her up to date.

Amongst all those beautiful puppies, Maria fell in love!
Oh Mummy, look at him, he's gorgeous, look at his beautiful little ears!!
Where have I heard those types of words before?
Well, I needed a male like a hole in the head; I think I have said that before too.
Filigranovij Farfor Wolkowo or Filip as he is known, it means beautiful piece of Dresden China, arrived with Berk, his wonderful father, his breeder and Edith Titse, who had bred Sapphira, the day before Crufts March 2008.

They had driven without stopping, except to let the dogs out, from Slovenia to here.
I had my beautiful baby boy. We bonded immediately. Helena left the morning after Crufts and Filip was left without his father and his breeder, he never looked back.
Filip's success in the show ring has been amazing, he has been a constant winner to date, including his very first show, the Borzoi Club open show, just a couple of weeks after he arrived here.

This is at his first Championship show, which he won.
His greatest win to date, was winning his class at Crufts this year.
Filip as I write this, is now 4 years old. He has only not been placed once, every other time and there have been many, he has been in the line up. The last show for him this year, he won his class and received the RCC, his 4th.
I am incredibly proud of him, but more important , his temperament is just wonderful, he hasn't got an evil thought in his body. I remarked on this to a breeder here, she said, of course it would be, all this breeders dogs have a wonderful temperament, they are all delightful just like she is. How true, this I know, she is a dear friend to me.
Since I became ill, this wonderful dog has certainly changed, he doesn't want to be away from me, pressing against me whenever he can. He is my comforter and his love has helped me through many a dark time.

Chapter 20. Sophie's Story.

Towards the end of last year (2010), after the death of Frost , I rang her breeder to tell her the sad news and at Martin's suggestion, I asked if she needed a home for one of hers. At first she said no, and then said, well I have a bitch, but you won't want her, she is 7 years old! A few days later we were on our way to Devon!

We spent the day we arrived, meeting her and getting to know her. Oh! She is pretty, she had been rehomed before, how anyone could have sent her back I just can't imagine. She has been nothing but perfect since the moment we had her.

We picked her up early the next morning, had a good 4 hour drive home. She was perfectly behaved all that long way. We let her into the house, took off her lead and she went straight to her bed and lay down! There has never been a moments trouble with Filip or Choo. She loves her walks, her breeder had said she was not a good feeder. I have had to cut her food down, she was putting on so much weight. I have shown her once in Open Bitch, as there was no Veteran class and she came a worthy second. She is dearly loved by all.

I hope there will be many more exciting things to write about this beautiful girl.

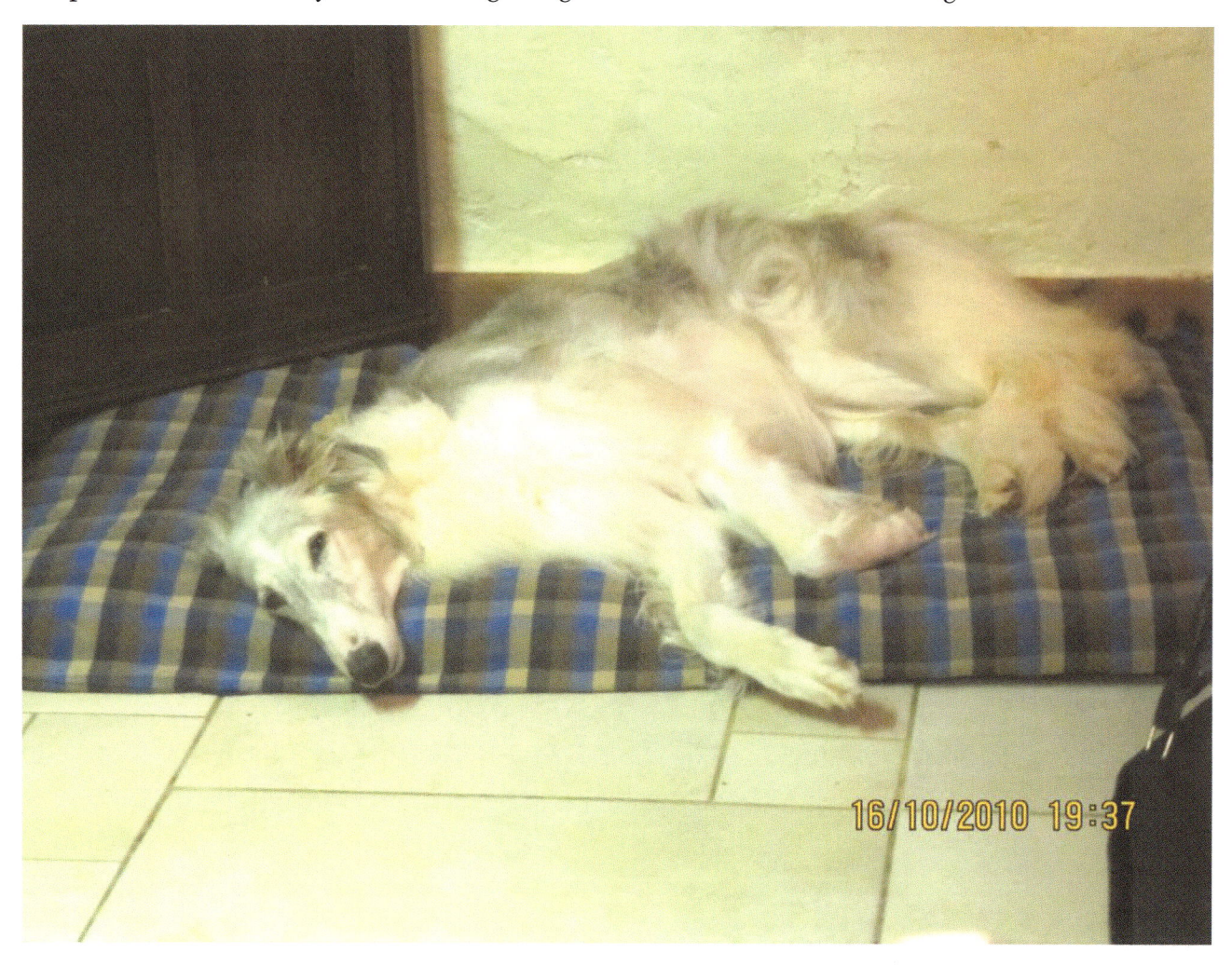

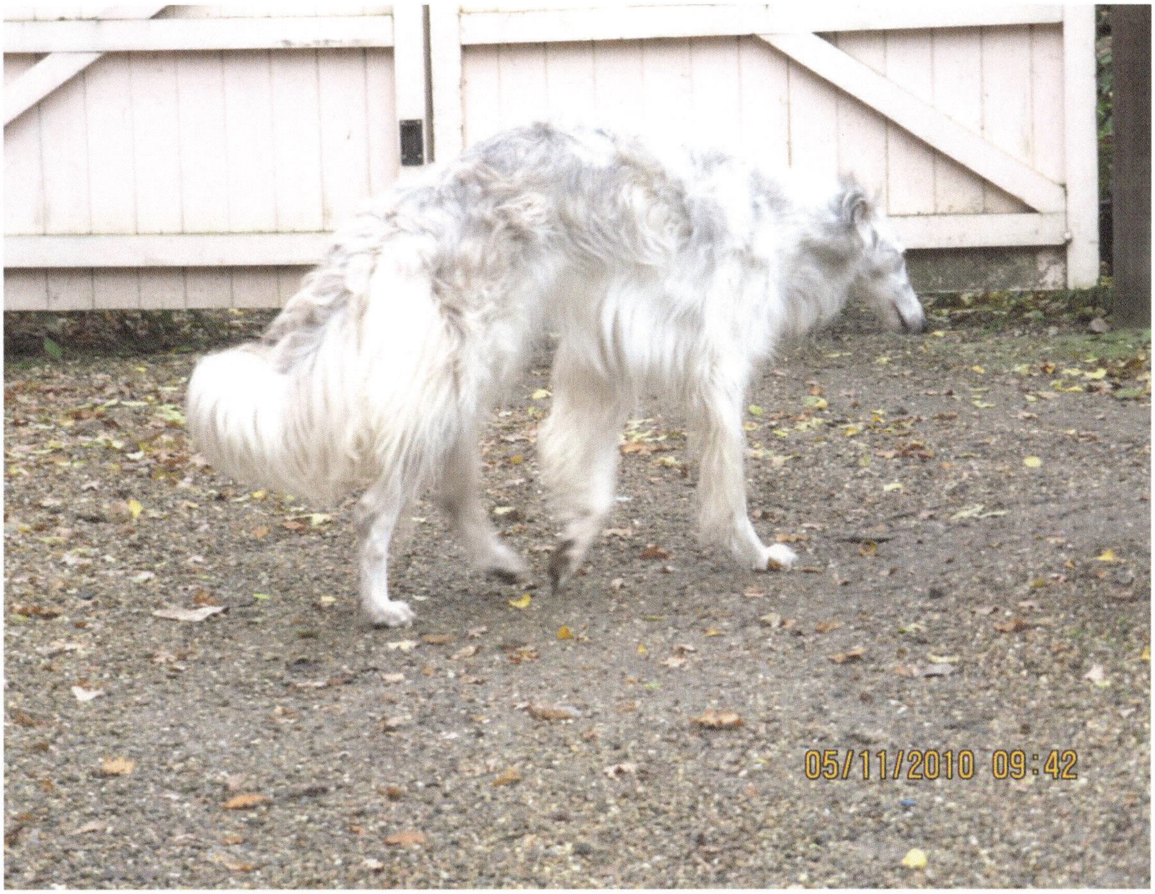
05/11/2010 09:42

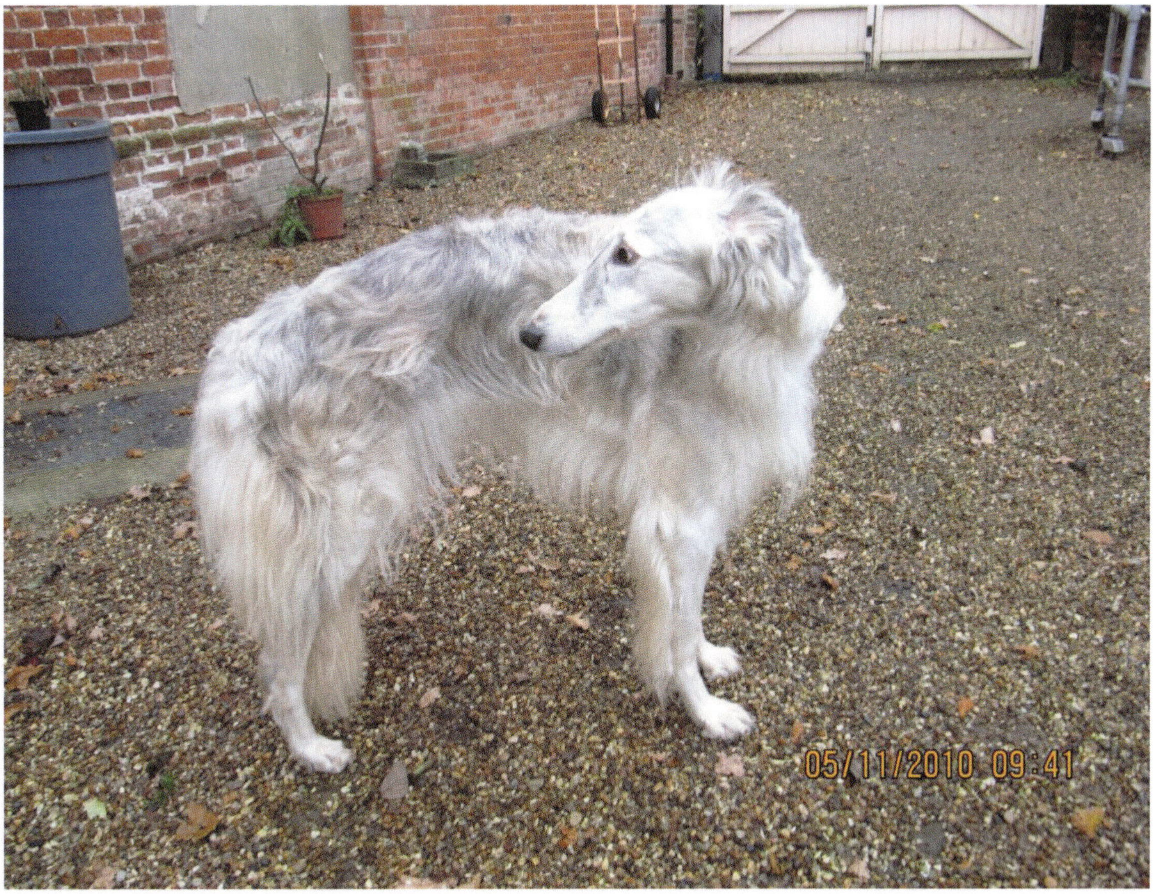
05/11/2010 09:41

Chapter 21. My Obsession

I was becoming totally obsessed by this breed! No longer was it good enough for me to have them as my beloved companions, I had to have more. I decided I must go to Russia, their homeland and know them in their rightful surroundings.

Lady Luck was on my side and she dealt me two beautiful and unexpected cards. I knew my late husband was not impressed with this idea and certainly, would not have come with me. I found the thought of arriving in Moscow, totally on my own, knowing no one, extremely daunting, in those days, very few Westerners visited Russia, besides, having got there, where would I look for a Borzoi?!

One evening, in the spring of 1990, some acquaintances came to supper with us. The conversation turned to Moscow. "I would love to go there" I said, ignoring the look I got from husband. "So would I" replied Anne. "I was in MI 5, but had to leave in 1960 and have recently been given clearance to return, shall we go together?" My dream had started and there was nothing my husband could do about this! We decided to go in the winter, to see Moscow, with the snow on the ground and agreed on early January 1991. A long time to wait but, Borzoi Heaven was in sight. Then, the second card was dealt. A few weeks later, reading one of the dog papers, my eyes fell on a small paragraph, "Anyone wishing to exchange information on Russian dogs, for breeds in England, please contact Anna Mikhalskaya, at this address". I couldn't wait! Off went a long letter to Moscow, telling her all about my Borzoi and, that I was proposing to visit early next year. About a week later, I received a telegram, "On receipt of this cable, please telephone Moscow-----
-"I can still remember my nerves, as I dialled that telephone number! A woman's voice answered, it was Anna, who spoke perfect English. Half an hour later, I put the telephone down, my heart was singing, my Russian Borzoi was within my grasp.

Crufts that March saw me going to the Kennel Club stand and arming myself with every breed standard they had!

I was to learn much later, from her mother, that Anna had received over three hundred replies to her article. She only answered one!

1990, dragged slowly to a close and early in the New Year of 1991, we set off on the great adventure. We did it in style too, flying Aeroflot, so we felt Russian from the start!

I do have to admit, that arrival in Moscow, is a daunting experience. Clearing customs and immigration took forever.

Our hotel, when we got there, was very austere and we were stared at as curiosities. However, a couple of vodkas soon put us right. That was the first shock though, learning there was no such thing as a bottle of tonic water! Something we both learnt to get over very quickly!

It was unnerving too, to find an armed guard on each floor of the hotel. I certainly locked my bedroom door every night.

The food was terrible, until we struck really lucky. With the help of an obviously crooked waiter, we learnt that if we signed the bill, for a main course and a coca cola each, which never appeared, we could have as much caviar and vodka that we could cope with. Needless to say, we eat in our hotel, whenever possible!

I have to say, my friend Annie, was wonderful, compared to one afternoon at the British Embassy, where she relived her memories, the entire week was given up to me and my eternal search for Russian Borzoi. A more long suffering and generous lady, I do not know.

Her introduction must have been horrendous for her. We had arrived in the evening and, the following morning, at 10 am, we were to meet Anna. What had not been made clear to us was the fact that Russians were not allowed to enter a tourist hotel. We sat in the entrance hall of our hotel, until well past the meeting time. I was beginning to despair that Anna had changed her mind but, I had noticed a lady continuously being refused access, so I went out to investigate. This was Anna. Within a few minutes, we were in her car, on the way to the Botanical Gardens and Tarik, my Borzoi adventure had begun.

Chapter 22. Meeting my Dogs in Russia.

What a culture shock this was!
We skidded and slided on several inches of frozen snow, at great speed, driven by Andrew, Anna's husband, through the streets of Moscow, until we arrived at the perimeter of the Botanical Gardens. Then, not through the main gates did we enter, but through bent iron railings, that just about allowed us to squeeze through, what have once been wonderful gardens, signs of topiary hedges, collapsed hot houses still remained. I do not know the acreage, but it must have been vast. Thick snow, freezing cold, but I had arrived; I was, with my dogs in Russia. There must have been at least ten, running loose, what a moment!
Then we met Tarik, I have to say, once seen, never forgotten, he more resembled a bear than a man! Enormously huge and hairy, but, what a character, half Georgian half Russian, a big drinker, a big laugher, a really jolly man, who loved his Borzoi with a passion. He had in all, I would think, about thirty dogs the conditions he kept them in, were something I found very difficult to accept, but then, this was
Moscow, not centrally heated England. To be fair, they are Russian dogs!

It was just so cold, a lot of snow, about eighteen inches and, everything was frozen solid. This included the dog's food, which appeared to be some sort of raw whole fish, mixed with a small amount of bran, or maybe, crushed up biscuit. The latter was hotted up on an open fire, and then mixed with the frozen fish. The dogs appeared extremely hungry and bolted it down in no time at all.
It is hard to tell just how many dogs he had there. At least seven ran loose in the Botanical Gardens and more too kept in small pens, with some sort of wooden kennelling, possibly a further ten, which included a litter of puppies.
He had about ten hunting Borzoi, coming from just two lines, one native to Russia and the other Swedish/Finish; the Russians were the finer of the two, looking a lot like ours. The Finish were bigger and courser. All the dogs were short of coat and some had bald patches and blotchy skin.

These dogs were a number of colours, nothing different to anything here; there was an exceptionally pretty bitch of seven, who was pale grey and white. She attached herself to me, leaning against me in the usual manner and putting her front feet on my shoulders. I would dearly have loved to have brought her home with me. He also had a very elderly grey dog, who I think was "my bitches" father – he was twelve years old, he was very shaky, his poor old hind legs looked as though they would not hold out much longer – felt deeply sorry for him.

The dogs all possessed fantastic friendly natures and, obviously adored Tarik. Yes, they were thin but they were regularly hunted and, obviously very fit. I feel certain that they accepted this harsh climate. They knew no better, unlike a few spoilt Borzoi back at home. This is what I had come to see, I had achieved another ambition!

Apart from these Borzoi, Tarik also kept several Hortje Borzoi, reminding me of large whippets and one Steppe Borzoi (Sredneaziatsky Borzoi) and several other dogs native to Russia, including one most attractive sheep dog that was native to Northern Russia.

I found these variations very interesting, as I had never seen them before.

Poor Anne, I think she must have been bored stiff!

Eventually, it was suggested we went into the warm, Anne and I couldn't have agreed more, we were both frozen.

The "warm" turned out to be a caravan, where Tarik lived in the middle of the Botanical Gardens. Nothing wrong with that we thought, until we got inside. Oh my God, what a smell!! A mixture of bad fish, sweat and human excrement. I really thought I was going to be sick. I lit a cigarette to try and cover the smell, only to be told, Tarik didn't like the smell of that, … well!!!

I turned to Ann and said I didn't think I could stand this, "Of course you can, remember you are British", came the sharp reply!

I think this picture really shows, how hard she is, "remembering she is British"!

The room was minute, a table in the middle allowed just enough room for three wooden dog benches around it. The cushions on the benches had definitely seen better days, a few fur coats were thrown over the benches and we were invited to sit down. Anna, Andrey, Tarik, Anne, myself and another man (who was to remain totally silent for the entire tea party) and a young girl, all squeezed round the table.

A large tea pot and some huge cups and saucers soon arrived, I made the big mistake of looking inside the cups, they were filthy! I do wish I hadn't, going on the theory, what the eye doesn't see, the heart doesn't grieve. My heart certainly grieved, every swallow was a nightmare, with the tea constantly threatening to return! The tea was poured, very strong and very black. I decided not to put my glasses on to study what was floating on the top of my mug, I just prayed it was tea leaves, but then, I forgot everything; out of an old cardboard box came the most wonderful collection of photographs – Borzoi hunting, Borzoi coursing, Borzoi killing, lovely dogs, lovely horses and wonderful scenery. These pictures at a guess must have been twenty to twenty five years old; the Borzoi were hunting two different quarry, firstly the hare, bigger than ours, weighing around six kilos and secondly, a fairly heavy antelope. In both cases, the dogs were shown being either slipped as are our coursing greyhounds, or hunting in pairs.

Tarik then told me through Anna, who was interpreting, that he was starting the Borzoi hunt again with the wolf; he had backing from the "Central Hunting Union" and the "Union of Hunting and Fishing in Russia". They already had a few horses and he hoped to have his first official hunt to coincide with the Moscow Show, in June of this year. He was extremely ambitious over this project and hoped to build the hunt up favourably with the past. I was later to see photographs of the trials towards this goal and I have to admit to feeling somewhat unhappy about it. According to the photograph, the trapped wolf was placed in a small pit with just it's head and front legs showing; the front paws were tightly bound together and tied to a pole, another pole had been put into the animals mouth, and a muzzle was tightly bound around the pole and then to two stakes at the side of the pit. The poor animal was probably tied behind in the same way, but it was not possible to see that on the picture. When the time comes to release the wolf, a rope is tied to one of it's hind legs, with a heavy piece of wood tied to the other end to slow him down; the reason for all this, I was told, is because the Borzoi had lost the instinct to hunt the wolf, so the prey must be made easier to catch. I was told, in the case of this particular wolf, the animal "lived". I wondered what happened to the rope and the wood. I was assured that the wolf hunting instincts would soon return to the Borzoi and that these unpleasant methods would stop – I hope so.

Tarik is also interested in the show dog and is involved in the Moscow Show. He is friendly with Galina Zotova, and is keen on her blood lines, he is hoping she will be judging the Borzoi at the Moscow Show this year, but he explained, she is not too popular as she is keen on her own blood lines and not the heavier Finish dogs, which many people own. He tells me she has judged in Sweden, Germany and the USA. Tarik has two nice carved plaques on his wall which he had won for "exhibition", also, an attractive water colour of two running Borzoi, and a lovely head study of a Hortje.

I was told by Anna that a Borzoi in Russia, can now sell for as much as 3,000 roubles, about £500. Tarik himself would never sell a dog, only give them to approved homes.

My memories of that day amongst those beautiful dogs and wonderful scenery, will stay with me forever, it was a quite unforgettable experience, not least of all, the lovely grey bitch.

So the time had come to go and goodbyes were said all round and then, the "totally silent man", opened his mouth for the first time, "Not at all" he replied in the plumiest English accent to our thank you very much; Anne and I looked at each other, and fell about laughing! Then it was a breath of glorious fresh air, off through the snow, through the Russian gate, the way we arrived and back to civilization and another world.

So ended my first meeting with the Russian Borzoi.

Chapter 23

The day was far from over though. The next was to be very different.
Andrew and Anna took us to a block of high rise flats. After climbing what seemed endless flights of stairs, we arrived at the home of Natasha Zucova, and her three Borzoi, Champion Marysha and her two daughters.

Marysha was seven years old here and was the winner of the Moscow Show, Kiev and Union Show, which was held once, every fifteen years.
Her daughter's, litter sisters,

Markyza, has two diplomas in 2nd grade and Mazzirka, are two years old.
What a contrast from where we had just come from! This flat, was warm and comfortable, the dogs, family pets, a joy to see, happy and contented girls, reminding me of home.
We spent a couple of very enjoyable hours there, with Anna translating all the tales of Marysha's considerable show success. Their pride at her winning the Union Show would have been clear, without an interpreter.
Simply, I loved it!
Then we were off again, to my final meeting with Russian Borzoi.

This time, another block of high rise flats and the home of Irena Studenckina, who was at that time, a dresser for the Bolshoi.

Her flat was identical to the last one, the same size and warm and comfortable. She also, had three Borzoi.

Melissa, who is described as "very good in exhibition in Moscow and regional shows and has five diplomas of the third degree, her daughter, Panipasckha, born 1989, described as "very good in youngest group and also works well on hare". I know that she went on to become a Russian Champion.

The white bitch is Grisha, bred by Tarik from his famous dog Barun.

This bitch certainly has a far more comfortable life here, than she would have done with her breeder! As far as I could see, they lived a life of luxury.

This was a very comfortable flat; we were plied with vodka, cakes and biscuits, the latter two being difficult to obtain in Moscow in 1991.

After that feast, we were offered some wonderful chocolates, I am a chocoholic and couldn't resist! To this day, I feel embarrassed and ashamed, chocolates in those days in Russia, were a rarity and the height of luxury. Oh, how I wished, when I found out, I had not been so greedy!

Anna was wonderful to Anne and me, she spent the next two days showing us the sights of Moscow, it was beautiful and we had a wonderful time. In these few days, our friendship was sealed. To this day 2006, we are still in touch, sixteen years after I answered her article in the dog paper.

All too soon, we had to leave Moscow, catching the overnight train to Leningrad, as it was called then. There were six people in our overnight sleeper, two were English, who had been to the Moscow circus and had seen Borzoi's performing, that was the nearest I came to my wonderful breed again before I got home.

We did have one amusing incident, if rather unnerving, in Leningrad.

We decided to take ourselves out to a restaurant one evening. It was situated up several flights of stairs, so we took the lift. On arriving, we went into an enormous room and were given a table for two, beside the dance floor, where we also saw a fantastic cabaret.

After a while, we decided to order another bottle of wine. I had been aware of a table next door to us, with two men sitting at it. The action of ordering more wine had a drastic affect. The men picked up their table and placed it along side ours, our order was changed from wine to champagne, which we could not stop them paying for. I sensed trouble; we were clearly being picked up! I saw the band returning and whispered to Anne, we should get the hell out of here! Too late, the good looking one grabbed Anne and I was stuck with a fat greasy one! They turned out to be a couple of second hand car salesmen from the Urals.

By this time, I could see that Anne was beginning to panic too, when we sat down at last, at the end of a dance, we caught each other's eye and, without a word, made a run for it! To our horror, we realised they were coming after us. "For God's sake, don't get in the lift" I said. I think we must have broken all records on that decent of at least five floors, we could hear them behind us. Reaching the ground floor, we shot outside, where luckily, there was a line of taxis waiting by the door, we jumped into the first one, slamming the door, shouting our hotel address. We drove off, just in time to see them running toward our taxi. What a relief, somehow, I don't think they were running after us, just to escort us into a taxi!

We also had a very interesting morning at the Hermitage, where in their gift shop, I managed to buy a Borzoi model. That made my day!

My first taste of Russia, how wonderful it was, but certainly it was not to be my last. I just knew I had to return.

Chapter 24. The first Return.

It didn't take me long!
Early in 1992, I received a 'phone call from Anna, asking me to go to Moscow in September, to judge Borzoi at the Moscow Military and Hunting Show. I do not judge, so I asked if I could put a friend forward in my place, which was agreed to. Pam was really excited about this, it meant she was the first English person to judge Borzoi in their homeland. We asked another girlfriend to come with us, then we decided we should take a couple of men with us, for support.
So, in September of that year, five of us boarded our Aerophlot flight to Moscow. We were met by Anna, after the usual lengthy procedure at passport control and customs.
She took us to a reasonably comfortable hotel, which was obviously guarded by the KGB; several uniformed men stood inside the main entrance and kept a strict eye on the comings and goings of all who entered. After they got used to us, they were pleasant enough and I, always on the look out to feather my nest, discovered one of them, was an extremely good caviar supplier!!
Nothing much had changed, each floor was still guarded by a surly uniformed female, our bedrooms were sparsely furnished and I still locked my door at night.
Early the next morning, Anna arrived to take us to the show. We were amazed; the showground was on a military air base. It just seemed incredible that Oh, so secret Russia should allow this.

The whole thing was quite fascinating, not just the military side of it, but the appearance of unfamiliar breeds of dogs,

The Estonian Hound, used for flushing out quarry.

The Russian Gonchi, used for the same purpose.

The attractive Hortje I had seen the year before at Tarik's

The Tazi or Middle Asian Borzoi.

And the Laika.

There were some sad sights too, or maybe it is because we are not used to them, but I wasn't too happy with this.

The little thing and several others were for sale. I cursed our quarantine laws. There were a few eye catchers though, such as this!

A car sun screen, really needed too, it was a hot day.

Another thing I really liked, were the medals awarded to winning dogs.

I thought this a lovely idea and much more interesting than our rosettes.

Chapter 25. The Borzoi

When we first arrived at the showground, there was hardly a Borzoi in sight, but slowly, they started to arrive, firstly in ones and two's, then in large groups. Pam had a big entry, all curious, no doubt, to see what an English judge would do.

Pam had an entry of well over one hundred Borzoi, stretched over two days, dogs the first day. At the end of each class, every owner and dog, lined up to hear Pam's verbal critique, unlike us, who, if we have won or been placed second at a show, wait patiently for the dog papers to arrive and read what our judge has said about our dogs. In a large class, of which Pam had many, it must be extremely difficult to say something that will not upset the owners of those near the back and last, in the class!!

Her critique was translated for her, and I imagine she must have done a good job, as nobody looked like hitting her!

The organisers of the show provided lunch for us, which we had picnic style, in the Borzoi ring.

That was fun and gave Pam a break from judging.

She picked her eventual winner from the Open Dog class, of fifteen entries, as she did her bitch winner, Open Bitch, a class of seven. .

Here, the dog winner lines up with the bitch, for Best of Breed on the second day, the BOB, going to the bitch.
It was then, that Pam was in for a shock!! She was coolly told she would be judging Afghans, Greyhounds, Hortje, Taigan and Tazi. The latter three, of course, she knew nothing about! Anyhow, all went well and everyone seemed quite satisfied with her results.
After Pam's judging had finished, we wandered to the far part of the showground, where a track had been set up and Afghan's and Borzoi were racing to the lure. It was good fun to watch,
but I found the pictures particularly interesting, with the military planes and the train in the background.

At the end of the first day, we were taken from the showground by Anna and Andrew. At this point, they seemed to be minus a car. We walked a few yards, until we came to a busy street, when, nothing daunted, Andrew flags down the first mini bus he sees, removes the driver, gets in his place and we all pile in. Usual in Moscow?

We were driven to the flat of Irena and Igor Kovischnikov. It was the most beautiful flat, overlooking the Moska River, where a great many cruise ships were moored, a beautiful sight, but it was the sound, as we entered the flat, that was the most beautiful of all. Igor was seated at a grand piano, playing this moving tune and singing to it in Russian, it was eerie, beautiful and haunting, without knowing what it meant, I wanted to cry.

This is the translation:

I have never imagined that one could fall in love so.
I never realised that in my soul there dreams a passion,
I can't now understand that it could happen so,
That now I am mad over Borzoi, both in dreams and in reality.
Yes, yes, I have fallen in love with these very Russian Borzoi,
Which in the old times were kept by Aristocrats and Tzars,
But the storm had come and with the White Guard,
They were gone away and perished,
Pursued as all the past as the symbol of Monarchy.
For the Russian Tzar was mad on them as me.
The Wolfhound hunt was so loved by officers
And that is why the dogs were to be done away with and shot.
But, every sunset is followed by a sunrise and so
I have faith in my dear Russia's Renaissance
And every defeat is followed by a victory
And let us together thank the soul of Russian Borzoi.
My friends the Slavs, open your eyes and be at last awake,
And having forgotten your troubles for a while,
Have a good look at Russian Borzoi
The crown of your land.

Igor Korshunova 1992.

How true this is for me. I hope it is read at my funeral, it sums me up completely.

How strange is this too? Why do I love Russia and its people so much? Is it just because of the Borzoi? I doubt it. Or is my love of the Borzoi, because of this?

My father, a racehorse trainer, was asked by the Tsar, to go to Moscow as his private trainer. Sadly, I do not know the year, but obviously pre 1917. He was not married to my mother at the time, but his then wife refused to go. Thankfully, or presumably, I would not be here, writing this. His story of this, coupled with my mother's dog Ivan, must have helped.

It was to be years later, as I have said earlier, I was the only one who Anna Mikhalskaya replied to, amongst a great many letters.

Her mother, Nina, was to say to me, when she was staying here, a few years after we had all met, how strange it was, that mine was the only letter that Anna answered, and as we talked, she felt our lives had been parallel, that, maybe, in another world, we had been the same. I do not really believe this way, but … … … I cannot dispute the depth of my friendship with Anna.

Irena and Igor gave us a wonderful meal, plenty to eat and drink, in their very comfortable flat, which possessed some very nice paintings of Borzoi hunts.

We were all sad to leave, when the time came, we climbed into the hijacked minibus and Andrew drove us back to Nina's flat, where, to our horror, there was an enormous meal waiting for us! How I wished I had not eaten so much at Irena's! What a spread Nina put on for us, including caviar, I managed to find my appetite!

Chapter 26 The Miracle.

We returned to the showground for the second days judging, I was sitting in the Borzoi ring, watching Pam judge, when out of the corner of my eye, I saw Olga, who I had met previously, at a show in England, when she had paid us one of her many visits.

While Pam was judging, Olga, suddenly rushed up and said, "Would any one like to go to Perchino"? Would we? Wow!!!! How she did it, I will never know!
At 6 am the next morning, a mini bus arrived outside our hotel, Olga, her Borzoi and 5 very excited people got in. We drove for a good hour into the suburbs of Moscow, when we suddenly pulled in to a tenement block of high-rise flats. "What are we doing here?" I say, "You can't go to Perchino without the Borzoi" Olga answers. With that, 5 people emerged, each with a Borzoi and all climbed into the minivan. By this time, we English feeling that we had been starved of our breed, irrupted in delight and we settled down to a three hour journey to Perchino. Except, we didn't really!! There was a massive black male on board with us, in charge of him, was a slight Russian girl, who didn't seem to have too much control over him. He was everywhere and if he could have eaten us, he would have done and I mean eaten, not bitten! It was enough to make these English Borzoi lovers slide down in their seats! The minibus had to stop half a mile short of the village, as the road would not take vehicles, so out we pilled and walked the short distance.

When we entered the village, people came out of their houses to greet us, many in tears. Olga translated. We were the first people, Russian or foreigners to have visited Perchino since 1917.

We were all so moved. We visited the wonderful church, where Nikolai once worshipped, with the wonderful engravings on the walls of the hunting horn, that we now use as our Borzoi Club

symbol. All completely derelict and so sad, the Borzoi hospital, the whelping kennels, the latter two, now both houses. So much emotion, so much atmosphere. The house itself, so magnificent

in its glory, raised to the ground. Absolutely nothing remains. The Revolution did a complete and thorough demolition job. The villagers surrounded us, touching us, tears on their faces; they hugged the Borzoi, all crying, as we were, Olga translating. Then she said, there is a very old man here, who is sick and we are going to get him to meet you. He was the son of the chief kennel huntsman of the kennel. He had been a small child and had witnessed the destruction of Perchino; he had seen both his parents and his siblings shot, and all the dogs and the horses, by the white guards. He came out, a withered looking old man and very small and frail, when he saw the Borzoi, the tears started to fall. We all felt overcome, and then we went into shock! The 6 Borzoi were all there on their leads but he headed straight to the evil big black male, we English all gasped in horror. This just goes to show, we do not know enough about our breed. He went straight to him, no hesitation, tears pouring down his face, threw his arms around the dog and buried his face in his mane.

The evil one lifted his head and turned towards him, so gently did he caress his face, licking away his tears. I have never known the old man's name but I call him "The Spirit of Perchino". Afterwards, there was plenty of vodka drunk, to the past, to Nikolai and to the futer of Russian Borzoi, the "Jewel of their crown".

I don't remember ever having felt so much emotion, being the first people to go there since 1917, taking the Borzoi with us, it was just so amazing

and yet so sad. That beautiful house, raised to the ground, what a waste, what a tragedy. I imagine it must have been filled with beautiful furniture, pictures and porcelain, probably many items relating to the Borzoi. The wonderful hunting parties that took place there that often included foreign Royalty and dignitaries. The magnificent horses stabled there and above all, the finest Borzoi in the country.
All that is left as a reminder are the two overgrown willow trees that once stood so proudly either side of the fountain. .

It was with a heavy heart, that we said our goodbyes to the wonderful people of Perchino and walked past those willow trees, back to our bus.

Our day was not over yet though, unknown to us, our Russian friends had packed a wonderful picnic for us.
The bus pulled off the road and parked beside a large wood, Wolf Wood, where once the Perchino Hunt had hunted. This amazing picnic was laid out for us. What an effort they had been to, food was still very scarce in Moscow, there were all sorts of cold meats, eggs and bread rolls, plenty of butter, vodka, brandy, coffee with milk and sugar, even tinned dog food for the Borzoi. I have a very nasty feeling that these kind people probably went short of food for the next few weeks.
It was a truly wonderful picnic, with Olga translating, with the help of the vodka and the brandy though, we suddenly all seemed to understand what everyone was saying! There was much laughter, the Borzoi were all loose, galloping across the fields, chasing each other, just as they must have done in the past.

It is moments like these, when even the "Evil One" became friendly, that I wonder, are they aware of the past and the great dogs that had galloped here before them. Did they sense spirits of long ago, the great wolf hunts, the reason for their very existence?

I will never know, but I do like to think they did.
So, our wonderful visit came to an end, a day that will stay in my heart forever.

Chapter 27. The Perchino Hunt

Thirty kilometers to the west of Tula, on the banks of the Ula river, was the Perchino country estate, built as long ago as the reign of Catherine 2nd (the Great) by the famous banker Lazarev. At the end of the last century (19C) the estate was acquired by Grand Duke Nicholas and has since become the leading nursery in the country for breeding genuine Russian hunting dogs.
Perchino was the place where outstanding Russian Borzois were raised – Russian and Anglo Russian hounds which were exceptionally ferocious with their quarry and which had a splendid exterior. Dog breeders came from Germany, France, Belgium and America to watch the hunt and acquire good dogs. Through the work of cynologists and simple Russian sportsmen – hunt leaders, handlers and huntsmen – the traditions of correct breeding of hunting dogs have been preserved. Nowadays pedigree work has reached such heights that it can be called an art, and a lot of attention has been paid to the beauty of the dogs. According to eye-witnesses it was a sheer delight to watch the Perchino Borzois racing or to listen to the rising and falling of the hounds voices.

The memoirs of a leading huntsman, V.D.Solontsov, who took part in hunts in Perchino, have survived. This is how he describes this marvelous sight:

"The picture was thrilling in its beauty; first of all a pack of red hounds with the leading huntsmen and handlers, flanked on both sides by mounted borzoi handlers with dark coloured borzois in pairs (17 pairs), lined up in front of the onlookers, followed by a pack of skewbald hounds with 18 pairs of skewbald and light – coloured borzois; it was like an echo of better times long ago when the ringing sounds of the horns called the hunt to order; people and horses stood as if rooted to the ground, and pairs of amateurishly assembled dogs gathered around in various poses. The whole picture, lit up by the rays of the setting sun against the background of the countryside, exuding a kind of extraordinary strength and charm which only a huntsman would understand. We stood there in silence and our imagination was swept away to the autumn fields and woods where the intrepid pair of hounds would soon descend like a whirlwind, the whole pack baying in unison."

Hunting with Borzois and hounds was organized by peasant sportsmen, the leading huntsmen and handlers. Michael Mamkin, Efim Alexzanova, Peter Kuleshov and the huntsman peter Vasiliev were the real magicians of the hunt. Their experience of leading Borzois and hounds is even today of exceptional importance to huntsmen.

The Perchino hunt consisted of two packs of hounds with 45 in each pack, (one pack red with dogs of Russian blood, the other light bay and skewbald of mixed blood), 130 Russian hounds and 15 English Borzois. Every year at Perchino up to 60 Borzoi and 40 hound puppies were weaned. According to A.P. Uspensky's description, the leading huntsmen and handlers who worked with the hounds were dressed in red half – kaftans belted with black straps. They carried daggers with white bone handles in their sheaths. The leading huntsman's kaftan was usually sewn with gold lace, his white lambskin hat had a red top and behind his shoulder he carried white nickel horns chosen for their sound, on a black cross – strap.

The Borzoi handlers were dressed in thin kaftans, belted with a black strap with a sheath dagger and black blue – topped lambskin hats, and carried a horn on a cross – strap slung over the shoulder. The grooms had half – kaftans sewn with gold lace.

The Perchino hunt was led by a black skew – bald Russian hunting Borzoi, a dog called Strike from V. P. Voieikov's hunt mentioned by E. E. Dryansky in his "Sketches of a Nobody".

In 1876, a pack of hounds was acquired from the Rayazan huntsman Obolyaniov, and from Baron G. E Delvig, two brace of harlequins and a sandy skewbald dog called Snatch, who excelled in his ferocity with the quarry. Delvig's hounds were descended from Zapolsky's marble - white harlequins, famous in Tambov province.

These hounds had a keen sense of smell and were excellent wolf hunters. Then the famous Borzois of F. V. Protasev's Ryazan hunt were bought - Single, Dash, Slant, the bitch Roxane and two grey – skewbald dogs, Baryshnikov's Boa and Lodyzhehnsky's Strike.

In 1887, red colored hounds were acquired from P.F. Durasov which where descended from A. I Arapov's dogs, famous in Penza province. The blood of Anglo – Russian dogs from I. I. Sokolov's hunt was mixed with Delvig's harlequins via the light bay – skewbald dog hound Batyr, who was descended of old Glebov dogs from Rakhamaniov's hunt and hounds obtained from France and England. A light bay – skewbald pack which excelled in its keen scent and marvelous voice was bred from these dogs.

At the same time, in 1887, nine red coated dogs descendants of the Arapov pack, were bought from N.A.Panchulidzev. Their blood was mixed with that of the famous hounds' of P.N.Belousov, N.V.Mazharov and A.A. Lebedev.

In breeding Borzois, all attention was given to the ferocity and friskiness of the dogs. Pairs were chosen from these qualities.

In1890, a sandy skewbald dog, Fling, was acquired from the famous Boldarev Russian hunting borzoi and in 1891, the pack was supplemented with the sandy skew-bald dog Gladden, which was superbly frisky and marvelously built. Mating Gladden and Glory produced some faultlessly frisky Borzois.

In autumn 1891, the sandy grey hunting dog Tender, unrivalled in character and friskiness, was bought from B.A.Vasilchikov. From Tender and the sandy grey bitch Blizzard, some very good litters were obtained, dogs such as Falcon, Fierce, Tender 2nd, Lady, Madcap, Arrow, Rout, Shoot, Antelope and Orphan. Falcon was especially outstanding and won a gold medal at the Moscow show, coming second after V.N. Chebyshev's famous Reward.

Rout was extraordinary frisky and would catch any wolf over rough ground.

In Blizzard's pedigree were the famous Borzois of P.M. Machevarianov and N.V. Nazarev.

A big influence on the development of pedigree Perchino Borzois was Tufty2nd, bought from P.F. Durasov. Tufty and Blizzard gave dogs of the same type: Lout, Barbarian, Witch and Blizzard, primarily dark coloured dogs.

In 1895 the red skewbald dog Sorcerer, remarkably thin, with a steeply rising back and thin little ears, was acquired from B.A. Vasilchikov. Mating him with Dove produced the famous Borzois Proud, Ruffian, Storm and Terror. In 1897, using blood pairing, Sorcerer's offspring's were paired with tender's and Tufty's offspring. The result was splendid and gave dogs exclusively of one type. Sorcerer's son Diamond - an outstandingly beautiful dog – won a gold medal at the Moscow show as well as the prize for the best hunting borzoi. Diamond's son, the marvelous grey – skewbald dog Quick, was sold to America.

Excellent results were also given by mating Perchino Borzois with those of M.P. Ermolov. The blood of Perchino Borzois went into many pedigrees both in our country and abroad.

Russian breeders as far back as the last century proved the need for

Type 3 – 3 blood pairing, which is when an outstanding common ancestor is found in the third generation of both dogs and bitches pedigree. Dogs were chosen strictly according to patterns.

The famous expert and author of a book about the Perchino hunt D.P. Valtsov wrote: " … ancestors of dogs which became part of the Perchino kennels were from the same root, which is how I personally explain the appearance in the Perchino kennels of dogs of the old type".

All the best blood at the time, from the hunts of P.M. Machevarianov, N.P. Ermolov, F.V. Protasev, S.S. Kareev, A.V. Nazimov, S.V. Oserov and N.A. Boldarev, entered the Perchino Borzoi's pedigrees.

D.P. Valtsov, the former hunt steward, wrote a book, "Hunting with dogs at Perchino", which gave some unique descriptions of the Perchino hunt: " …"2nd September 1899. The Perchino hunt had spent the night in railway wagons at the Dvoriki station, about three miles from the "Bear's Forest", which belonged to Count Bobrinsky; At ten o'clock in the morning, pair after pair emerged in a long column and went through fields to the island, followed by the main pack. They walked in a column because, before the island where the litter of wolves is, there is no hunting allowed, due to fears that the wolves might be frightened by the noise, moved and driven to the edge of the wood.. The island described as a rectangle, with shorter sides to the east and west and longer to the north and south; The eastern side looked out over a deep transverse ravine, on the spur of which, in a westerly direction there was a broad strip of young forest of pines and oaks. The hunt stopped before it reached the unwooded ravine; the pairs lined up in two columns and went to occupy the northern and southern sides, the last pairs having closed on the western side. It was a quiet grey autumn day; dotted around the fields were stooks of corn which had not yet been gathered, and which provided good cover for the pairs of dogs. I stood on a raised hill and could see almost all the pairs; the island seemed from where I was looking to be lying in a gentle sloping depression, and to the north the field ascended into quite a steep hillock, at the top of which, there was also some pairs standing behind stooks. Hardly had the pack, which immediately caught up with the adult female, completed a circle around the island, when the adult male ran to the hillock towards the handler Michael Eletsky. Michael had the red – skewbalds Zairka, the daughter of Emolov's Seize, Strike, the son of the Perchino Barbarian, and Flutter, the son of Dubrasovsky's Tufty with him. Having waited for the quarry to reach him, this experienced huntsman let the dogs loose as soon as the adult male glanced to the side towards D.D. Osipovsky, who was standing nearby; Michael's frisky dogs immediately got at the adult male wolf and went head over heels with him, having missed seizing hold of him; the wolf jumped up but Osipovsky's dogs with two of Nazimovsky's breed had arrived with some haste and met him; the wolf trampled one of the dogs but Michaels dogs had regained their feet and again covered him, pinning him to the ground, as another of Osipovsky's dogs went for his throat; just as people hastened up, the wolf suddenly through off all the dogs, broke out of their circle and, having thus separated himself from his pursuers, ran at full pelt back towards the edge of the wood; the dogs willingly gave chase, but to catch an adult male, running to the forest edge, is only a job for ferocious and exceptionally frisky dogs. It was now that the Perchino pack showed it's worth in this respect: Zairka flew like a bird ahead of all the other dogs, made a dash for the wolf and hung on his haunches, thus shortening his stride; Root and Flutter seized him by the scruff of the neck and again forced him down, and a moment later, Michael was already lying on him and tying him up. Hardly had I looked away from this scene than further to the left, the adult female ran to L.A. Shakhovskoi's pack, noticed that the dogs were dashing towards her, turned towards V.K. and ran off so quickly that she managed to turn away from four dogs that were trying to cut across her, but not very much, so that all the dogs had to set off in pursuit. It was fine to see how quickly Diamond, Seize and his brother Whirlwind, (a gift to Prince Shakhovskoi) began to move towards her, and they had only a short way to go to gather for the attack, when the Grand Duke's groom's sandy dogs, Falcon, Antelope and Falcon Hen went at her with such keenness and caught her such a blow shoulder to shoulder, that she was knocked over, the dogs covered her and she was tied up. The whole pack led the horses to the hillock, but the handlers overtook the hounds in the fields, stopped them once and drove them back to the leading huntsman who was already blowing his horn at the edge of the wood: "Here, here, he-e-r-e!"

I have seen a lot of hunting by the most ferocious dogs with blood from the Nazimov and Novikovsky kennels and the adult wolves have always got away in such circumstances; once he had torn himself free after two attacks near the edge of the wood, the adult male never allowed himself to be caught, especially across a heavy field, and here as well, my heart missed a beat: "He'll get away!" but the friskiness of the Perchino dogs again came to the rescue: the red bitch from Golovin's pack, Siren, flew out from the group of dogs, made a spurt awesome to behold and caught the wolf, hanging on to the nape of its neck, the dogs covered him and raised him up in the air at Golovin's feet as he jumped down from his sleigh. It was a very large adult she-wolf. A third wolf, fully grown like the first one which had been caught, poked his nose out at Koshelev's sleigh, but at once went back into the ravine and got through his pursuers, back to his island.

It would take me too long to describe all the hunts for adult wolves; 56 were caught in the Perchino hunt, and some hunts were more beautiful than those described, but I have chosen on purpose, various years and various dogs, so that the hunters reading my story can be sure that daring and ferocity are characteristics of the breed as a whole, rather than one or two dogs chosen at random".

Chapter 28. The Near Tragedy.

The following day, a days hunting was arranged for us. Various cars drove us to Tarik and the Botanical Gardens. where a large army type truck was being crammed full with Borzoi and

Hortje, men, women and children. Far far too many living creatures in there.

I just don't know how they didn't see the danger, that it was a hot day, that there was no air-conditioning, no windows to open and worst of all, no contact with the drivers cab.

The truck led the convoy of about four cars, through some interesting countryside and some pretty villages. We had been traveling for some considerable time, when the lorry came to an abrupt halt. There had been so much banging and shouting from the back that eventually the driver heard. He jumped out, raced to the back of the truck and pulled open the doors. What followed was horrendous, the dogs poured out, engulfed in a cloud of steam, desperate to get fresh air. The inside of the vehicle had become a furnace; children were crying and women screaming. Then we saw the worst disaster, one of the Hortje's had collapsed. I thought he was dead and turned away in horror. The two men in our party jumped out of their cars and grabbed the dog. "He's alive" they screamed, luck was on our side, we were in a small village and right beside us was a water butt. Between them, they lowered the dog into the water, after what seemed an eternity, with me carefully not looking, I heard a shout, "He's coming round". I opened my eyes to see him feebly struggling on the grass.

After a while, he seemed strong enough to continue the journey, but this time, in the car. The dogs and people climbed back into the truck and it set off again, this time, with the back doors open.

Not long after that, we arrived at our destination.

To our horror, Tarik wanted the Hortje to hunt, with one voice, we English all cried "NO"! Oh! How glad the dogs were to get free of the lorry, they galloped wildly,

A wonderful sight! It was a relief to all of us that that journey was over.

The next thing, was tuition for the English, first of all how to use the slip
leads, nothing like as easy as it looked and a great source of amusement
to the Russians. Then we were each given two Borzoi, I looked around and realized that there was going to be an awful lot of walking, there is something about the Russian skyline, it seems to go on forever.

From the start, things didn't go too well! The first tragedy was Pat, who stubbed her toe, she kept walking, but was obviously in agony. When she got home, she had it X-Rayed, only to find she had broken it.
The next was Richard, who was given two of Tarik's dogs, all they did was constantly look for their master and tug hard in his direction, making it very difficult and tiring for him.
I was certainly right about the walking, we lined up in one long line and

walked for miles and miles, we were all totally exhausted and to make matters worse, we never even caught a glimpse of a mouse, let alone a hare or a fox! My first Borzoi hunt was not exactly a memorable one!

A couple of remaining memories, both of evenings out.

The first a restaurant the five of us decided to try. We had a pleasant meal, with dancing and a cabaret. I remember, it was an enormous room, the far side of a vast marble hall. It was from this hall we heard a gun shot. One of our men bravely went to investigate, on his return, he suggested that we left, we agreed. On approaching the hall, we women were advised not to look, so of course we did. There was an enormous pool of blood on the floor and blood was still dripping down the white marble walls, we were certainly all very pleased to get out of there.

The second memory is lovely. We decided we should take Olga out for a meal, as a thank you for taking us to Perchino. We told her to come to our hotel on our last evening. She looked at us in amazement and reminded us she would not be allowed in. We made sure she was, she got a few strange looks, but nobody was going to say anything, as long as she was with us.

She kept looking round the hotel in wonder; it was lovely just to see her expression.

We found a restaurant that was quiet, gentle and warm, just what we wanted. Oh! I wish I could describe the look on her face. We had a lovely meal and we were all so happy. Then a flower seller arrived and we clubbed together to buy her a bunch of flowers. Her face was beautiful, her eyes filled with tears. "This is the first time anyone has ever bought me flowers". It was magic, one happy little girl.

So ended another amazing Borzoi experience.

Chapter 29 The Rescue.

Jim, who had been on that trip with us and I, talked long and hard about the state of some of the dogs, particularly Tarik's in Moscow.

We decided we must do something about it, talking was just not good enough.

So we set about fundraising to buy food and veterinary products.

We contacted all the well known food companies, asking them to donate bags of food, we went to our veterinary surgeons and asked for out of date medicines and vaccines, we pestered our friends for cash donations, infact, we were a perfect nuisance, but it worked!

We managed to collect a great many bags of food from the companies we approached. The next problem was how to get it to the docks, for shipment to Moscow, with very little cost.

Jim contacted a great many haulage firms, with no success, they all wanted full payment, until he tried Eddie Stobart. No problem, we will take it for free. There are some nice people out there.

Jim and I fixed our date for our return to Moscow and, early in January 1993, we met up at Heathrow, to catch our flight to Moscow.

My first sight of Jim, had me in fits of laughter. He was standing beside a trolley that was piled high with boxes and packages; I remember the top one resembled a large hat box, "What on earth is in that"? I asked, "[1000] worm tablets" he replied. Tied to this box, was a large placard proudly announcing in large red letters, Russian Borzoi Rescue. We did get some rather strange looks and I couldn't help wondering, how many people even knew what a Borzoi was!

We wheeled our trolleys to join the queue for the Aerophlot check in. When we eventually reached the desk, we found we were being checked in by a very surly British Airways lady. We placed our rather large amount of hand luggage on the desk to be weighed. She looked at us with a completely expressionless face and in a cold voice said, "That will be £400 for overweight". We gasped, "but this is a rescue mission" said Jim. "£400" she curtly said. Jim had a fairly short fuse and I could see it was about to blow, the argument was getting louder and louder and this woman was not going to budge.

From behind us, a man appeared from nowhere and put an arm on Jim's shoulder. "How are you?" he asked in a heavy accent. It was the Russian Ambassador!

He turned to the surly woman, "There will be no excess baggage charge, and furthermore, these two will be upgraded to first class." Revenge was sweet indeed and first class on Aerophlot was the height of luxury!

We were even sorry when we arrived in Moscow, having sustained ourselves throughout the flight on free caviar and vodka.

Dear Anna was there to meet us and drove us to her mother Nina's flat, where we were to stay throughout our short trip.

As usual, their hospitality was wonderful but sadly, I can't say the same for the rest of our stay. The sacks of food taken by Eddie Stobart had arrived safely, but the customs refused to release it unless we paid them £500. Something we definitely were not going to do.

I remember sitting with Jim and Anna for hours and hours, day after day, in a stuffy office, while Jim argued with them, to no avail.

At one point, a young girl was brought in, to take down all the details of the food, how much there was, what it was and why we were doing it.

She sat at an 1850 style typewriter and proceeded to take the details, typing slowly with one finger!! It was exasperating, so much so, that Anna finally lost her temper and saying something in Russian, which I imagine was pretty rude, pushed the girl out of the way and took the details down herself.

Sadly, it was all to no avail and a complete waste of our time. The Russian customs would not give in. It was not until several weeks after Jim and I had returned home, that we heard through Anna, that realizing they were not going to get any money for the food, they released it.

So, I suppose in the long run, it was worth all those boring hours!

It was bitterly cold in Moscow in that January. Jim and I visited Tarik in the botanical gardens and we were horrified at the frozen conditions and the state of the dogs. Everything, food, water was frozen solid, the only means of thawing anything, was to light a fire and place the food or water in a large cauldron on top of it.

A somewhat lengthy procedure.
The younger dogs and the hortje, were feeling the cold and were dreadfully

thin, this is a borzoi puppy, about two months old; it was heartbreaking to see it.
There were many more kennels there than there had been on my earlier visit, stretching a good way into the Botanical Gardens, but it was made clear to us, there were others which we were not allowed to see.

The kennels, which were wooden and double tiered, were extremely small, with small runs.
Of the dogs themselves, as I have said before, they were in extremely poor, condition, lacking in muscle, with no excess flesh what so ever. The maximum across the backs was between two and a half to three inches. It has to be said though, they obviously adored Tarik and had wonderful temperaments. It had to be a hard life for both them and him.
Jim and I were certainly glad to be taken into the warm! What had probably been a large summer house in grand days of what must have been once, beautiful gardens, was already filled with several people. Food was provided in the shape of bread and cheese and something that looked like rather overgrown gherkins. Someone then brought in a tin bowl, filled with finely sliced raw meat. Anna informed us all that it was leopard's tongues!
There was an immense amount of laughter at this, we could only presume and hope, that it was all a joke. Jim and I declined to try any!
Plenty of vodka though and the room was beautifully warm, so much so, that someone opened a small window, almost immediately, a beautiful blue/grey borzoi stuck his head through it, I longed to let him in but it was not allowed. That saddened me, his eyes seem to be begging to come in.

After a time, Jim nodded off on a bed that was in the far corner of the room, I had had enough by this point and made a suggestion to Andrew that I would like to go somewhere to buy some caviar. What was to follow, was yet another amazing experience.

Andrew led me across some frozen and very slippery streets, into the back entrance of a butchers shop. There, amongst at least a dozen frozen cattle carcasses hanging from giant hooks and several fierce looking people, all holding butchers' knives and giving me very strange looks, I was abandoned. It seemed like an age, I was certainly very uneasy and was desperately wishing I had woken Jim up and made him come with me.

Eventually, much to my relief, Andrew returned, carrying a box with the biggest tins of caviar in it that I had ever seen! I had enough money on me to buy six, so six I bought. As far as I can remember, they were only about £10 each. Now, even the smallest tins are about £40.

I do regretfully say that eventually some weeks after I got home, my daughter and I opened the final tin, horrors of horrors, it had gone bad. I really believe I must be one of the very few people who have fed caviar to their Borzois!

So, another visit had passed, I only hope we had helped, now, ten years later, I believe we did, maybe not physically but mentally. In an e-mail, early in 2006, that I received from dear Anna, telling me how appallingly Tarik had been treated by someone he knew and trusted, she mentioned this visit, saying how grateful the Moscow Borzoi people were and that they would never forget what we did for them. I have to rejoice in that. Rejoice that in our own small way, we helped to give a few Russian Borzoi and their owners, a little comfort.

Chapter 30 The Moscow Show.

June of the same year, saw me back in Moscow, this time with Richard Duckworth. The renowned Russian judge and Borzoi breeder and veterinary, Galina Zotova, was judging the Borzoi and Richard was invited to judge some specialty classes, which was nice for him and he was kind enough to let me join him on this brief weekend.
We arrived at the showground early in the morning, where it was already getting hot. Galina was in the ring waiting to start her judging, I was clasping a large box, filled with veterinary medicines that I had scrounged from my vet and friends with half used medicines, syringes and bandages.
I knew from Anna how impossible it was for Galina to get medical supplies and, how distressed she was over this.
I walked in to the ring, glad to have got there before judging began and handed her the box.
She gave me a hug when she saw me, but when she opened the box and saw the contents, tears of gratitude fell down her face.
Galina does not speak any English, but the Russian words poured out of her. I will never know what she said, but I knew by her expression, how delighted she was.
Galina had an enormous entry of Borzoi, it was becoming very hot and people were sitting around under trees with their dogs trying to keep them cool. In Russia, showing is hard work; you walk round the ring continuously, until it is your turn to be gone over. A large class, with twenty to thirty dogs, means an awful lot of walking!

Richard and I were fascinated by the amount of people walking round the ring, smoking a cigarette, something that would not be done in this country

The majority of the dogs, despite the hardships of those times, looked extremely well, but what impressed us was the beautiful Russian heads

I saw several dogs that I recognized from the Moscow Military and Hunting Show, where Pam had judged the year before, including her best Bitch and B.O.B. What a disappointment, this lovely bitch looked tired and bored and had put on a great deal of weight.

I was really sad to see her like this, then I learnt to my horror, she was in whelp. Poor bitch, she should have been left at home, particularly on a hot day like this.

Then, joy of joys, I saw this big black male, the "Evil one" from Perchino, looking magnificent. I have to admit, I do not know where Galina placed him but, he came under Richard later that day and got Best of Breed.

It was a thoroughly enjoyable day, with a lovely happy atmosphere. It was also interesting too, seeing so many unfamiliar breeds there. I saw the Black Russian Terrier for the first time, now of course, they are a familiar sight here. What I really loved were the medals, this little chap looks so proud.

A short but happy stay in my beloved Moscow.

Chapter 31 The invitation.

On the 12th of September that year, my poor husband died of that cruel disease; it was a happy release, but never the less, devastating.

Dreadful for my poor daughter, as he died two days before her birthday.

How my friends in Moscow got to hear about his death, I don't really know, I can only presume through some of my Borzoi friends in this country.

In those days, we did not have e-mail and I had letters of condolences by fax. These were shortly followed by the invitation. I was invited to go to Moscow and hunt with the Cossacks, what an invitation, what a dream, my beloved dogs, my beloved country, my Russian friends.

Since my first visit to Russia, this had been my dream, but was this the right time? I felt very shaky and unsure of myself since Mac's death and needed to be surrounded by familiarity, the thought of taking myself off to Moscow was at that time, very daunting.

Discussing it one day with a girlfriend, Barbara, she thought the whole thing sounded wonderful and offered to come with me. This seemed the answer; the thought of going on my own was daunting.

In those days, you could not visit Russia privately without an official invitation. This I obtained and at the end of October, visas and flight booked, Barbara and I set off for Moscow.

We stayed the first night in the flat of one of the organizers and, the next day, we were put on a train, for the fourteen hour journey to Alexicovo, in the Novonikolaieski region, about 300km from Volgograd.

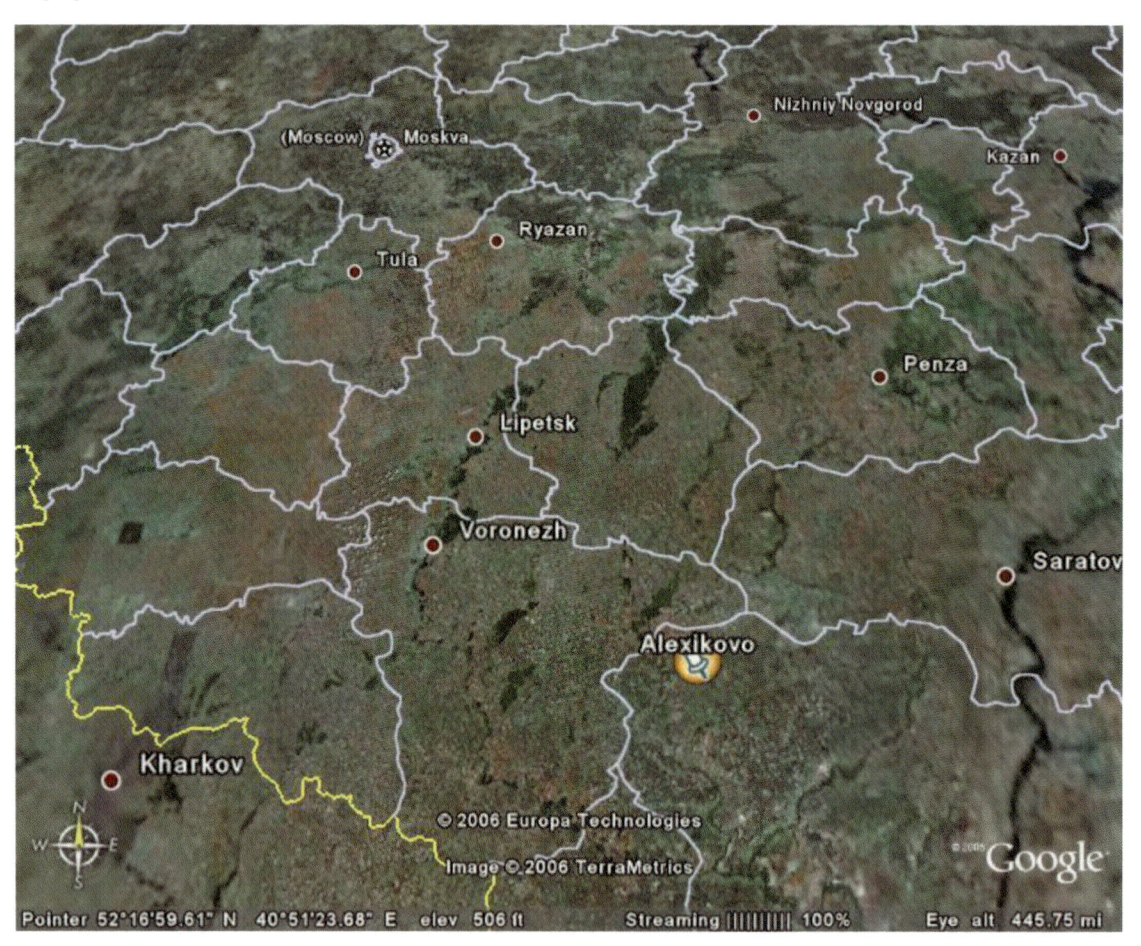

We shared a sleeper with the two smart hortje mentioned earlier and their owners, a friendly couple, who spoke reasonably good English.

The train was incredibly hot, I felt sorry for the two dogs, obviously distressed by the heat. Their owners did their best, every time the train pulled into a station, they would rush outside with them, walking them up and down the cold platform, sometimes with heart stopping results, as the train would be pulling out as they scrambled aboard.

Smoking was not allowed in the carriage, in those days both Barbara and I were smokers, so partly to get away from the heat and partly to relieve the boredom, we would stand in the small passage way, between two carriages, puffing at our cigarettes.

We did try and get some sleep, but it was so hot, it was virtually impossible.

Eventually, around four thirty a m, we pulled into a station, where we disembarked into the freezing cold, which served as a great relief after the heat of the train.

We were met at the station and driven to the Cossack camp, a journey of about thirty minutes. Here we were met by Tarik, (does anything to do with Borzoi in Russia, ever take place without him?) Today, he had eight Borzoi with him and three Hortje. Several other Cossacks were there with their dogs, who we were introduced to, and at around nine am, they, the dogs and Barbara and I climbed into a rather clapped out truck, and drove to the "Meet".

We arrived some half an hour later, at a farm belonging, I was told, to one of the oldest living breeders of Borzoi. The sight was unforgettable; here was the beginning of my dream come true! Several more Cossacks mounted on their sturdy ponies, all wearing the inevitable fur hat, very glamorous, carrying their long thronged and beautifully made leather whips; I was to be presented with one later in this adventure. The ponies' saddles and particularly the bridles were extremely ornate, covered in tassels and silver medallions and of course, all with their Borzoi.

We started hunting around 9.30 and continued with the odd short and very necessary break for vodka, until 4.30 pm. So it was a long day for dogs' horses and people.

At this point, I feel I should explain the rules and regulations of the hunt, which were firmly adhered to.

Each handler, be it he or she, on foot or on horseback, had his dogs on slip collars, three to a lead, and we would walk or ride in a straight line, across acres of open land, the edge of the Steppes. The quarry was mainly hare, a larger and lighter coloured specimen than that found in Britain. We also hoped to find a few foxes, and the possibility of a wolf had not been ruled out. The latter, to my relief, failed. I have always been passionate about wolves. The Borzoi who first saw the quarry, and only those, were slipped for the course, so depending on the number of dogs the handler had, there would be a minimum of three, but sometimes six or nine, coursing at the same time, What a sight to me, my breed, doing what it was bred to do, in the land of its origin, unbelievable magic, and the sound of the hounds still in line, baying to be released, to this day, echoes in my ears like music.

The courses on an average lasted ten to fifteen minutes. The hares did not seem to jinx like ours do, but ran in a straight line, until they eventually outpaced the dogs, or disappeared into woods or undergrowth.

The one hare that did twist and turn, was the only one killed out of about
Twenty, in three days hunting.

The dogs themselves were incredibly fit, showing hardly any signs of distress after a long course. They were extremely thin, but I am certain that was due to the amount of exercise they were having, than lack of food. If they were undernourished, they could not possibly have coped with the enormous distances they covered each day.

Concern was also shown over their general welfare.

On the third day, there was no hunting, to give the dogs a rest, and at camp at night, attention was paid to any cuts and sores that may have incurred during the days hunting. The dogs too, were always fed before us, although I have to admit, I never did see what they were given to eat. If it was anything like our food, it was of doubtful origin, very fatty but very filling, and I don't suppose the dogs cared!

The camp was a very jolly, happy place at night.

The food might have been a little suspect, but as I said, it was hot and nourishing and I found it quite enjoyable, maybe, helped by the copious amounts of home brewed vodka that I consumed. The food itself, was cooked in an enormous cauldron on top of a bonfire, and as far as I know, was left stewing all day, while we were away hunting.

The vodka, much the same, it was fermented on top of the fire, then strained off into bottles, after it had cooled,

It certainly had an amazing effect, a couple of glasses and everything and everybody became wonderful!

The Cossacks slept on the camp site in various huts, there was of course, no running water, if they needed the toilet, they disappeared into the bushes with a spade. In hindsight, I think it was infantly better than the situation Barbara and I found ourselves in.

This grim looking hotel was our home while we were in Alexicovo, it might look uninviting from the outside, but that was nothing to the horror of the inside. It was absolutely filthy, all I can say is, thank God we weren't eating there!

The only toilet facilities were outside, in a small brick building that consisted of a lavatory, with a small basin and cold tap. The stench was unbelievable and you could not get to the lavatory without wearing rubber boots. Barbara and I soon decided that washing was out of the question and whenever possible, we used a bush in the garden.

Our bedroom was pretty grim and I remember how hard the bed and the pillow were. We both felt we would much rather have roughed it at the Cossack camp, but fully realized that our hosts were only doing what they thought was right by us.

All this was a minor problem, when compared to the beauty and wonder of the days hunting. To be in that vast Russian countryside, watching these beautiful animals running, streaming in the wind. I found it so emotional and I realized how very lucky I was to have had this wonderful opportunity.

To think, without Barbara, I probably wouldn't have come, but this was just what I needed, it calmed my soul and gave me strength to face the futer. This was something Mac would never have considered doing and I was doing something without him, as I would have to learn to do, for the rest of my life.

The whole experience was a joy to me; everyone was so friendly to us. I think we were a bit of a novelty to them, two English women traveling all this way, to hunt with the Borzoi. Now of course, many foreign people travel to Russia, to do just that, but this was nearly fourteen years ago, and since the Revolution, visitors were practically unheard of in Russia. A few guided tours maybe, but two lone women, NO!

I used to enjoy all aspects of the hunt, not just the thrill of the chase, the many short stops that we had for vodka and the sandwiches that some one

had kindly made for us both and the end of the day, when we paused before our long ride home, to give horses, dogs and men a rest and examine them for cuts and other injuries in the fading light.

We were tired too after our long day, but it was a gentle tiredness, combined with a feeling of peace.

On the days we did not hunt, Barbara and I were entertained royally.

We were taken to see a stud farm of Orlov horses and a corral full of Cossack ponies.

Little did I know at the time, that this would change Barbara's life forever.

Seeing these horses, for her gave birth to an idea, to buy one or two and ride them home across Russia and Europe, to her own home in Suffolk.

The dream for her came true two years later. She did just that and life for Barbara changed forever.

We were also entertained in Cossack homes, one in particular comes to mind, apart from his Borzoi, he had an enormous selection of animals,

including these, which I believe are Coypu, but he insisted they were giant rats!
All too soon, our wonderful week came to an end, but my memories of this wonderful place, will never die. Now, all these years later, I still say, it was the most moving, wonderful experience of my life.

Chapter 32 The Diary

Jan. 95, and once again I had this feeling, I must go back to Russia, what it is about this country I don't know. It was over a year since I had been and I really was getting withdrawal symptoms. Yes I wanted to see my friends again and most of all, their Borzoi. So visa granted, flights booked, I set off on the 28th Jan, trying a different route this time as Stansted airport is less than an hour from me, flying KLM and changing planes at Amsterdam. This proved to be a great idea as I was looked after, and given a really lovely afternoon by Corrie and Herman Bastinck of the Stroganoff Borzois.
I also struck lucky, as a friend of theirs was selling his collection of Borzoi books and postcards, so I managed to spend some money early on in the holiday!
Arriving at Sheremetyevo airport Moscow my love for the country and its people soon took a rapid nosedive! Two and a half hours later I was still queuing to go through immigration. Never, never, I swore to myself, will I ever come here again. A surly official looked at my passport and visa, glared

at me and then at the passport, a movement that he kept repeating. "Of course there's a difference" I wanted to shout. "You'd look different from your photograph if you'd been standing in a queue for over two hours". Instead I tried a smile. Shouldn't have done It didn't work! Another 5 minutes and then, relief, the double thud of the official stamp and I'm through!

Wonder of wonders, my friend Anna Shubkina was still waiting for me, and off we went to her father's flat where I was staying, and a very reviving glass (or two) of Georgian white wine. My love for Russia began to return. Shortly after what Anna calls "my period of relaxation", I followed her through thick snow across a park to her flat, to admire her litter of Hortje pups. There were eight in the litter and were seven days old, a lovely sight. The bitch was doing them well and Anna was justly proud of them.

Jan 30th. This morning we rose early as we were driving down to Alexicovo and Cossack country, a trip of some 670 kilometers from Moscow, and an estimated ten hour journey. We were well equipped for the trip, with a generous picnic of mainly "Bush legs" eggs, bread, cheese and plenty of vodka, hot coffee etc. Now for those of you who are a little unsure what Bush legs taste like, let me explain that on a visit to Moscow by President Bush, he made several references to the amount of chicken legs the Russian people ate, so in Moscow now chicken legs are referred to as Bush legs! We ended up eating our Bush legs at a rather unattractive filling station waiting in a queue (again!) for petrol. This time the pumps themselves were empty and waiting to be filled, so it was a fairly lengthy stay. It would have been nice to have eaten a little further away from the diesel fumes, but nobody was prepared to take that chance in case we lost our place in the queue, and the pumps ran out of petrol again!

At last we were away, driving through the lovely countryside of Tula. Great Borzoi hunting country and country home of my friend, the very respected Galina Zotova. On we went through Tula to Ryazan, which caused me great excitement. I'm sure you will know of the Ryazan prefix belonging to Jean Clare here in England. "Ryazan!" I shouted excitedly. I have a bitch very closely related, being a daughter of Ch. Ryazan Laura. "Any chance of seeing the city?" "On the way back" I was promised. My heart leapt. Only a potty Borzoi owner could get excited about seeing a town that is renowned for its ugliness, just because you have a daughter of Ryazan Laura! Eventually as it was getting dusk, we arrived at Alexicovo and Peter the Cossack's home, and best of all, Peter the Cossack's Borzoi. What joy! Back with my breed again. I was given a flat adjoining the house belonging to Peter's son and new daughter in law. Where they slept I do not know, but I did feel sorry for them being kicked out of their home for me. There was a great attraction to the flat though, in the shape of Prince the Borzoi. He was allowed to sleep indoors, as he had come from a hot flat in Moscow. (They are hot, too) and Peter felt he wouldn't stand the extreme cold, which his other dogs to put up with, outside. I would imagine it was about 20 degrees below zero. This is a comfort that I bet he doesn't receive next winter.

Jan 31st. Today was beautiful, bright sunshine and blue skies with plenty of snow. A days hunting was suggested. I was thrilled, this was an unexpected bonus! We spent the morning looking at horses while we waited for the worst of the frost to come out of the ground. (This was fine by me, as breeding horses is my business). We then moved to Uri the Cossacks' about ten miles from Peter. A fairly hazardous journey, the car got stuck in snowdrifts on more than one occasion and a great deal of pushing went on. Arriving at Uri's (I had been to both these farms before), we inspected his Borzoi, horses, goats etc. It was here I saw a dog of great interest to me, I thought I had seen all the Borzoi variations, such as Hortje, Taigan, Tazi, and I have even been lucky enough to see a Steppe Borzoi, but this was new to me, a bitch so like her famous cousins, but short coated. She stood approximately the same height at the shoulder, and the head carriage was just like our dogs as we know them. I was told she was a Russian Hunting Borzoi, still to be found, although very rare in some parts of middle Russia. Some 30 years or so ago, an attempt was made to form a breed standard for these dogs, but the interest in the Borzoi and the Hortje Borzoi was reviving after their decline caused by the revolution, and the standard was never completed.

We retired to Uri's house, where there was much laughter and much vodka drunk, and Uri's wife produced a terrific lunch. (No Bush legs here!) Uri is a trapper by trade making a living out of furs. I was asked to look at the fur hats that he had for sale, one was outstanding, so I grabbed it   only to be told that one belonged to his wife!!

At last, lunch over, vodka drunk with Dutch courage to the fore, we were ready for the hunt. The conditions were not really suitable, as there must have been a good two feet of snow. We had approximately ten Borzoi, including the Hunting Borzoi, (and how she covered the ground!) Not the usual "slipping" with three to a lead, but it proved fun with two very good hunts after red fox. There was excitement in the air, too, as a wolf had been killed in this area just a month before, a great talking point for the Cossacks. Sadly, the bitch that had pulled down the wolf had recently died of distemper. Were they, I wondered, chasing each other round that great hunting ground in the sky, or was all peace and harmony, and the hunter and hunted were lying down together at the end of the Rainbow Bridge. The day was magic,,   these beautiful dogs in full pursuit of their quarry, galloping.   wonderful graceful movement flowing, stretched low, breath coming like puffs of smoke through the frosty air   giving tongue   music to the ears   horses galloping   the swish and crackle of the snow   Cossacks shouting   the thrill of the chase. The fox gets away, too much snow for the dogs. A rest. Cossacks dismount. Horses' sides heave, sweat dripping. Dogs return, sink exhausted into the cold snow, We laugh, the thrill of the hunt still in our veins; vodkas drunk, comradeship   the love of the Borzoi,   it is overwhelming.

As dusk begins to fall, we ride home. Horses, dogs, people, tired, weary but happy. For me it's magic. My dogs, their land. The hope for the future of Russian Borzoi.

Feb 1st. An hour's drive to meet one of the oldest and most respected of Cossack Borzoi breeders. He is 73 and has 7 adult Borzoi and 2 pups. In his youth, he kept a kennel 22 25 Borzoi, ` which has had a great influence on the modern population of Russian Borzoi. This was an experience for me. This was a Cossack different from the rest. A man with manners and dignity. A calm, gentle man. A man of, what must have once been of outstanding good looks l living in peace and harmony with the breed. His love for them shone from him, their love for him obviously returned, a mutual love and understanding between man and dog. Wonderful specimens   the best I have seen in this area. Well-bodied, coated, with truly wonderful heads. I could have stayed there forever. The peace was perfect.

Feb.2nd. We leave Alexicova. "Most important" I was told "We must be away by 5.30 am", the weather forecast was bad, and we needed plenty of time for our return journey to Moscow. At 4.30 am, I hug Prince and feed him, probably unwisely on Bush legs etc., but he seems so hungry, make my way through driving snow to the nearest toilet at the bottom of the garden, find the door totally frozen shut, retreat behind the hut and promptly fall into a snow drift. That wasn't there yesterday!

An aside, I should be used to primitive toilet facilities in this country by now and this one was no better, being a 5 minute walk from my bedroom across extreme icy patches and over thick snow. Having arrived at the "piece de resistance", opening the door was a major hazard, once accomplished I was presented with a freezing wooden seat covering the inevitable hole in the ground. One particular morning, I had navigated all these problems, only to find that the previous user of this glory hole had misfired! My first reaction was to retreat behind the hut, and too bad, but on reflection it occurred to me that I might get the blame for the "mess". So I negotiated the treacherous path back home on three successive occasions, to boil a kettle, and try to clean up the unpleasant problem with hot water. (Give me a dog to clear up after any day!) Sometime later on talking to Anna Shubkina, I decided to tell her about it in case I was still getting the blame. Her reply to my embarrassed story, "Oh Gay, why bother, in Russia this is usual and in winter it is no problem, the frost will take care of all things like this until the thaw"!

To return to the present, I extracted myself from the snowdrift and returned to my room, collected my luggage, hugged Prince again and sat down to wait I waited and I waited! 8.25am precisely, I heard a movement and by 9.15 a.m. we were at last on the road. The snow had become heavier and was coming down thick and fast. It took us the best part of an hour to reach the main road, a normal 15 minutes journey. The road to Moscow was hell. Cars were stopped everywhere, on the side of the road, in ditches, some just abandoned right in our path, but we made it! As we drove nearer to Moscow, conditions improved and around 4pm, we turned sharply off the main road. "Where are we going?" I asked. "To Ryazan" our driver said. I cheered; I had not dared mention it in these appalling conditions, my heart raced. I would really see it! The excitement was immense. On we drove, the country got flatter and duller. We pulled in for gas. "Ryazan district" said our driver, no queues here! I jumped out of the car and took pictures of a very boring view but, it was my beloved Ryazan! An enraged lady came out of the filling station, shook her fist at me and shouted some very angry words in Russian. I smiled, she raged and the driver intervened   we drove off at speed! An hour later, the great industrial town of Ryazan appeared, smoke belching from huge chimneys, hiding the skyline, and the blocks of uniform flats.

How hideous, but to me, beautiful. At least I have seen it, wonderful, wonderful Ryazan! Yes Jean Clare, I thought of you, and yes, you too Ch. Ryazan Laura. We stopped in a small suburb of Ryazan, I became desperate to buy a souvenir, something local, something of Ryazan. In the end it was vodka, Ryazan vodka!

We reached Moscow fairly late that night and Anna took me to my great friend Anna Mikhalskaya's mother's flat where I was to stay for the rest of my holiday. Warmth, love and hospitality overtook me. (As did the vodka)! "Where have you been," says Anna "we expected you in Moscow yesterday. Sasha is angry!" "Sasha?" I say innocently. "Yes, he intends to make a film and had planned it for today:' Now, Sasha is another story. A Borzoi owner who works for Russian television. Sasha is always threatening to make a film which never materialises, so I took all that with a pinch of salt.

A lovely relaxed evening, at home and at peace with my Russian friends. The phone rings, tranquility goes   Sasha. I shall be round! 40 minutes later, doorbell rings. Sasha. Hugs, greetings, peace departs! "The day after tomorrow we make film, be ready by 9.30am."

Feb 3rd. A free day, I have the chance to go on a troika, something I have always wanted to do. It was heaven! The horses were beautiful and the troika so comfortable, I felt like a queen swathed in furs. Off we went across the snow, beautiful blue sky, people skiing, children tobogganing, dogs running beside us, barking, laughter, a whole hour of this, through the most beautiful scenery, what joy. Then it happened! In the distance coming through a gate towards us came a man with two dogs running loose beside him. "Stop! Stop!" I shouted "Oh stop!" I jumped out, grabbed my camera and ran towards them. Gesticulating wildly at the dogs and then the camera. "OK" I asked, "Is it OK?" "But of course" He replied in perfect English "Do you admire the Russian Borzoi?" Twenty minutes or so later I had to be pried away. "Please come to my home tomorrow and see more of my Borzoi." Sadly, with Sasha's plans for my International stardom, time did not allow it, but I have his address, and next time I shall be there! As for the two dogs I saw, one was a very handsome male of three years, self-black, and the other his son of eight months, looking very like his father. My day was complete.

Feb 4th. 9.30 am. Sasha arrived on time   most unusual! I really can't believe what is happening. The car is outside, and everyone seems to be in such a hurry. Anna and I get into the car, Sasha drives and Tarik, as mentioned several times before, who keeps many Borzoi and is a great hunting enthusiast, sits beside him. We drive off, in my opinion far too fast; I am told that we must buy some vodka, which believe it or not, proves to be very difficult. There are literally hundreds of small booths selling alcohol along the roadside, but to buy from them now is considered dangerous, the Chechens have infiltrated Moscow and besides hiding the odd bomb in public places, they have been injecting poison into the top of the vodka bottles. The week before three people had died from this poisoning. Eventually we managed to find some in a department store and off we go. We drive for a couple of hours, to a beautiful country estate.

Anna and I climb out of the car, clutching our bottles. What a sight met my eyes! 20 30 Borzoi, at least four foot of snow, blue skies and bright sunshine, bliss! I have met a great many Russian Borzoi owners, but this lot were all new to me, but it's been the same every time, friendliness, welcomes, questions, offers of food and drink, and talk, talk about these lovely dogs. The filming starts, it is supposed to be a film on why people visit Russia; four hours later and about Take 199, I was beginning to wish I never had! At last a break! A wonderful meal was produced, lots of laughter, in fact I can't stop laughing, feel it might have something to do with the vodka!

Suddenly, very swiftly I sober up! Sasha says "Here is your horse now get on and gallop with the Borzoi! I am very middle-aged and it is ten years at least since I have ridden. The meaning of "Give Gay another vodka" becomes clear! I got on, I galloped, I rode with the Borzoi, I loved it. A truly great moment for me but, the best was to come   "William". At this point, I have to explain. For a year or two now, I have been in touch with an English lady living in the Arab Emirates.' Carol is big into rescue, being made a huge task by the amount of dogs coming from Russia into the Emirates, they nearly all end up being abandoned, or left to die, "Boiled to death" as Carol puts it on the hot tarmac unclaimed. Such is William's story a Borzoi puppy aged about 7 weeks, found by the roadside with two broken front legs. Williams tale, I hope will have a happy ending. He is now in the UK, being released from quarantine at the end of March and coming to live with me. I have taken many photos of him when I have visited him and as he has such distinctive markings, I have for sometime been circulating them around Moscow in the hope that some one might recognise him, but with no success. This time it was different! At the end of filming I produced the photos. Nobody had any doubt. He had come from the Ukraine ¬but best was to come, one woman recognised him, she was absolutely positive about this and she has promised to try and get his papers for me. I will not be able to register him, but at least I will get to know his age. So the search for Williams origin is over, and sadly, so too is my holiday.

A farewell party that night, old friends, lots of new ones, addresses, telephone numbers exchanged. "Come to England, stay with me". "Please take these photos of my dog's home, and show to Borzoi people in England". "Oh! Those wonderful Russian heads" How sad it is to leave, but, then I remember six wonderful friends at home, and a sad little boy soon to join us, and suddenly I need to go.

Feb 5th. Sasha drives me to the airport, sees me through customs. "Good bye, see you at the end of May". Yes you've guessed it, I am going back again!

Gay MacRae 1995

CHAPTER 33

Sadly, I never did go back, or at least, not in the Borzoi sense. I am proud to say though, that Moscow came to me, or at least in the shape of a television crew, sent by Sasha. It was fun, they spent the entire day here, filming my Borzoi and interviewing me, well, at the time I thought it was fun, that is, until I received a video copy of the film and my interview from Sasha … that was embarrassing, what a pompous little Borzoi know all I was! All I can say is, thank God it did not appear on our television screens. Even today, I cannot watch it without squirming!

I made a final fare well holiday with Annie, my original friend of "remember you are British" days. We sailed from Leningrad, now St Petersburg, down the Russian waterway, to Moscow … … it was beautiful. Our time in Moscow was short, a matter of a few hours, but during that time I was so honoured, Olga found her way to the boat to meet me, Sasha, who had been ill and said he could not make it, arrived unexpectantly and my dearest Anna came in from her dacha in the country. How proud I am to have the love of these wonderful people.

I think the way to end this book, is to quote from a translation from the Russian, entitled "Russian Borzoi".

" Russian Borzoi is a symbol of Russia which has long ago passed away, gone with the wind … But maybe – also a symbol of futer Russia?

The beauty of Russian nature, unbelievable richness and originality of Russian historical past – and its estate culture, its traditions, peculiarities of Russian natural character – everything is represented in the striking appearance of this dog, whose beauty has no equals.

It is hard to imagine the grandness and magnificence of the aristocratic hunts and the emotional fire in which the Russian estate owners treated their Borzoi. A good dog often cost whole fortunes and villages.

Everything is striking in Borzoi – its beauty and strength, speed and hunting passion, braveness in struggles with wolf, and at home - delicate and interesting behavior: during many ages these dogs were not only welcome in their master's room but also slept and ate with them.

This breed has been popular abroad for a long time; many dogs due to their cleverness and obedience won Obedience Certificates.

The old type of Borzoi was preserved by efforts of the Russian Ymperator Society at the end of the XIX – beginning of the XX century.

Russian terms reflecting Borzoi, peculiarities of their behavior and constitution, and Borzoi hunting terms are so numerous and differentiated that consists a whole dictionary, poetical and not understandable for a stranger.

There are two types of Borzoi now in Russia – decorative, representative (dogs with abundant beautiful hair, large, magnificent, but too delicate for real use; the breeding centers for these are in Leningrad and Moscow) - and working type, less striking in appearance, but with much better hunting qualities. (Such dogs are bred in some provincial Steppe regions).

The world that gave birth to Russian Borzoi has perished, but the breed continues to exist, preserving its peculiar features".

Thanks to Russian Borzoi, you have made my life complete.

And yes, it is true, it's Hard to be Humble When you Own a Borzoi.

Lightning Source UK Ltd.
Milton Keynes UK
UKIC01n0826111213
222784UK00007B/58